YOUR
BRAIN
IS
BOSS

Using mind power to develop influence,
creativity and work satisfaction

DR LYNDA SHAW

Your Brain is Boss
Using mind power to develop influence,creativity and work satisfaction
© Dr Lynda Shaw

ISBN 978-1-912300-04-4
eISBN 978-1-912300-05-1

Published in 2017 by SRA Books
suerichardson.co.uk

Printed in the United Kingdom.

Testimonials

'*Your Brain is Boss* offers fascinating insight into the psychology and science behind how business relationships work, and how to improve your own behaviour and that of your teams for greater effect. If you are ready to become truly influential in your market, this book is essential reading.'

Jo Haig, CEO fds Director Services Ltd

'Dr Lynda Shaw is *the* expert when it comes to understanding how your brain influences what you think, feel and do. Knowing how your brain works will give you that critical edge in the work that you do and decisions that you make.'

Jane Gunn, International Mediator and author of *How to Beat Bedlam in the Boardroom and Boredom in the Bedroom*

'I started to read this book thinking that I'd just flick through it and pick out a few things of interest. Wrong. Not only is this a well-written book, it is so interesting you just want to keep going. Even though the introduction says you can dip in and out of this book, you won't want to; you'll want to keep reading from start to finish.'

Graham Jones, Internet Psychologist, University of Buckingham

'This book is a must read for every executive, manager, business owner or individual who is keen on developing their career. As soon as we get close to neuroscience, we often step into a field which is only understood by senior experts. Trying to transfer this knowledge to our business world is difficult or even impossible. Dr Lynda Shaw's book is a game changer. Perceptions, conflicts, stress, emotions, communication, resilience – she shows us how our brain works and how we can most profit from it. Read it now before you go to work. You will never make the same mistakes again.'

Niels Brabandt, CEO of the NB Networks Group

'A great guidebook on the psychology of management, with good academic referencing for those who want to read more. It's refreshing to read a how-to guide that is both grounded in the reality of management and leadership work whilst being based on sound academic research.'

Chris Jagusz, technology services industry CEO

'A refreshing change from the approach of process re-engineering and methodologies. Looking at how businesses really function through the interaction and intelligence of people. Provides a valuable insight into the role of emotion in business and how it drives relationships and decision making.'

Peter Manning, CEO and Private Equity Chairman

'A really useful handbook for anyone seeking to improve the performance of their business by harnessing a greater under-standing of key lessons from the world of neuroscience and psychology. This learning is nicely translated into everyday scenarios we recognise and which constitute the challenges almost every business has to overcome to succeed.'

Bob Quick QPM MBA, CEO (Former Assistant Commissioner of Metropolitan Police Service, New Scotland Yard)

'I suspect the absolute power of the brain goes largely untapped for most of us and we give scant attention to its health and development, yet properly harnessed it can help us achieve so much more in our lives. If you are looking for a guide for how to change that put your trust in Dr Lynda Shaw and this book.'

Jeanette Makings, Head of Financial Education, Close Brothers

'Sound, user-friendly guidance for everyday business situations, presented in an accessible way. I wish I had read *Your Brain is Boss* years ago. I would advise anyone in business to do so, it's great to have common sense with science in one hit.'

Sarah Ward, Managing Director, Sarah Ward Associates Ltd

Contents

Introduction

When I originally set out my objectives for *Your Brain is Boss*, I wanted to create an upbeat business book which draws on my scientific background in neuroscience and psychology as well as my experiences in starting and running businesses. I wanted this book to be pragmatic, readable and fun – unlike many leadership and business books – and to break some new ground and bring alive areas such as emotional labour and managing feelings while at the same time suggesting easy-to-implement 'action steps' to improve performance. I trust that by the time you have finished this book you will find that I succeeded.

So, take a look at the quotes on the facing page. Thank goodness I did approach *Your Brain is Boss* with the objective of injecting some emotional understanding into business, because the quotes point to some disconcerting findings amongst many senior business figures. Far from the perception of senior management contentedly enjoying the benefits of their high offices, I found the level of discontent, worry and stress was high and some had a history of depression and anxiety disorders. It doesn't have to be this way.

I asked them what they were like when they first went into the workplace. Without exception, all faces softened as each person reminisced about how they had such great ambitions, how they were confident and how much energy they had. 'Those days were good days. I really thought I was going places. I'm sort of there, but it's not what I thought it would be like. It's so much harder,' said one.

Hard. A word the interviewees used a lot. 'It's hard to understand people.' 'It's hard to make good decisions.' 'It's hard to communicate.' And as for being the influential person they had always dreamt of being, lifted up on a platform of business successes and having a positive impact on all they met, well, that seemed like a million miles away.

" *I'm sick of board meetings where everyone nods in agreement, but no one actually does what they say they will do."*

" *I'm nearly 49 years old and I'm worried that younger people are nipping at my heels. I'm scared my skill set is becoming outdated and there is no budget for training."*

" *Where are all the good quality people? So many seem highly intelligent, but they don't actually add value."*

" *I'm working harder than ever, this fear of failure thing is killing me."*

" *There's loads more legislation, but no one communicates it effectively."*

" *I'm not interested in all that pink, fluffy, emotion stuff. I only want to make money and save money."*

" *The boss who genuinely values people is very special and guaranteed work for life."*

To make matters worse, their health and private life were suffering too. They felt disillusioned due to lack of promotion or poor business growth and it was hard to switch off. The person they wanted to become hadn't emerged, and it didn't matter whether they were just starting out in business or had been in business for a long time. Frustration happens at any stage, and it can be highly stressful. Stress is fine in small doses, but in the long run it can do a lot of damage.

Through my years of running businesses and working with clients, I see many anxious, stressed-out people who are not enjoying life. Business seems to stall when this happens, with employee engagement and customer satisfaction suffering badly. Time is the most precious thing we have, and when each day disappears in a blur of angst or inertia, we have wasted our time, and that time will never come back.

It's amazing, isn't it, but we have a genius for ignoring fundamental truths and over-complicating matters to the point of being overwhelmed. One of the goals of this book is to offer a *variety* of tools that can *simplify* your working and personal life so that you can achieve far more than you do at the moment. Simplification leads to clarity of thought, creativity, clear communication and stronger relationships, and it waves goodbye to ambiguity, misunderstanding and poor decision making.

That is what galvanised me to write this book. Based on neuroscientific research and psychological theories, I have pulled together a wealth of techniques for you to use to improve and develop you and your business and consequently make your life far more pleasant.

You see, when we put our brain in a pleasurable state we are the most efficient and effective we can be. For, although your brain is boss, you can decide what state you want your brain to be in. You can choose to take control and put your brain in an optimum state for health, wealth and great communication. That is the foundation of this book.

Read this book if you want to become more confident and resilient. If you would like to find yourself in control of emotion rather than emotion controlling you. If you want solving problems creatively to become second nature to you. If you'd like making great decisions to become an easy habit. If you want to communicate your ideas effectively, become better at listening to others, and to watch your business flourish. And if you want to become influential, someone to look up to.

Why? Because this is the way to become a successful business person. A high achiever, a wealthier, healthier person who achieves and maintains a position of leadership with a band of supportive fans. This means that you will become more valuable in the workplace, a more attractive option for embracing new opportunities, and you will enjoy being a person of influence.

This is not a step-by-step guide, because once you have mastered these techniques, you will have changed, so you could never revisit step one and work through the book a second time. But what you can do is acknowledge how well you have developed once you have finished reading this and work through the book more than once with a fresh new eye and new ways of seeing the same information. Or perhaps you could use it as a reference book and dip in and out where you see fit.

Whichever way you choose to read it, each chapter is easy to follow. All the stories and case studies are original as they either happened directly to me or I witnessed them first hand. The facts are based on solid research and the tips are tried and tested and I know they work.

The first chapter is about perception. This is an important start as it demonstrates there is no collective reality, there is only individual perception, and when we understand that, we can develop into discerning listeners. I ask you to read this chapter first, because once you have mastered these ideas, you will use the rest of the book far more productively.

To nurture and fuel resilience is the only way to be fit enough to deflect the curve balls. And life is full of curve balls. Take, for instance, time. There just doesn't seem to be enough time, does there? This is increasingly becoming a major problem as we constantly feel under huge pressure to get everything done. It would seem that no matter how much we know about managing our time, working out how to complete something before going onto the next without feeling overwhelmed remains elusive. When we are drowning in a never-ending to-do list it negatively affects our emotional and mental wellbeing.

Do you dare have time for yourself? How often do you turn off your computer? How often do you spend time for yourself without a glass in your hand, a cigarette or recreational drugs? All these carry risks for poor health in the long run. But there is plenty you can do that has been scientifically shown to alleviate stress and escalate good health and wellbeing. So the second chapter is about resilience and the advantages of meditation, and about how to meditate and practise mindfulness, ensuring healthy emotional and mental wellbeing.

While still on Chapter 2 we look at the constant health promoter – exercise. Some people love it, others hate it, but the evidence is overwhelming that exercise keeps us mentally sharp and socially happy and maintains our bodies in the optimum state for good health. And let's face it, without good health, our working life suffers, as do our relationships while we are preoccupied with trying to become well again. I can't think of a single person who welcomes ill health.

Later in Chapter 2 we discuss a subject that many are in denial about. Finances. When did you last look at your bank balance? Do you have a spreadsheet that shows all monies going in and out each month? Do you know at any one time how much you can spend without going into the red, without compromising your savings plan, without dipping into your holiday fund? Would you rather not know because it may make you feel out of control? Financial wellbeing helps eliminate fear. It helps you feel in control and a whole lot calmer. No matter whether you do not have enough money each month and struggle to make ends meet or whether you have plenty of money and worry about where to put it for growth and security, I promise you everyone worries about money at some point in their lives. So the final section of Chapter 2 will go over how you can achieve optimum financial wellbeing.

So, Chapter 2 is designed to elevate your confidence and resilience, two essential attributes if you are to thrive in an age of rapid change.

Moving on, Chapter 3 shows you how to develop emotional intelligence (EQ), emotional literacy and emotional labour. What does this mean? Basically, emotional intelligence is a skill that can be measured in terms of how well you recognise emotion in yourself and others and how you manage this. In this chapter, you will gain a brief understanding of EQ and learn the four core skills needed for excellent EQ. You will understand why this is essential for strong business growth and how to practise the tips on a daily basis until they become a habit.

The section on emotional literacy helps you recognise and manage how you feel, how you empathise with others and how you express yourself appropriately while staying in control. Both enable and empower how you go about your daily business.

Third, emotional labour influences the wellbeing of your employees, customers and clients. This section starts with asking what emotions your organisation requires of its people. For instance, how do you want staff or colleagues to regulate their emotions when dealing with customers? This seems straightforward, but if how employees truly feel is not aligned with how they are required to feel, internal conflict will ensue and they can become non-productive or perhaps unwell.

If you want to influence customers to buy your products, or to influence anybody in any context, remember that emotion drives their decisions. And not only that, some decision making may happen below awareness. This means that you must make sure – from the very first email, phone call or meeting – that you always treat people well.

Now that you feel empowered by improved self-awareness in these skills, it is time to polish up the way you solve problems, think creatively and make decisions. After all, you now have the tools to listen, empathise and use emotion confidently. So Chapter 4 works through methods for you to become more creative in the way you approach and solve difficult issues. Creativity is an essential tool in a world of economic uncertainty and inconsistencies, and one that will push you ahead of the rest.

Chapter 5 identifies the different ways we make decisions – heuristics, expert intuition, strategic thought, gut feel and so on. You will become familiar with the strengths and weaknesses of each and when and where to apply them. A step-by-step guide is offered at this point to facilitate structured decision making. Of course, there are times when making a decision is not the best option, so this will be covered too. You will also work on putting the brain in an optimum state to think clearly with sound judgement, a must for problem solving. Problem solving is an inevitable part of decision making, so learning to recognise real problems, and collecting data via observation, conversation and research, is the way to identify how to deal with situations, subsequently put actions in place and be open to effective feedback so that you can monitor the outcomes. All of this will ensure you are excellent at making decisions.

However, there is no point in making excellent decisions if you can't communicate them well. So in Chapter 6 you will double your impact and find a whole new world which outlines why fun should be taken seriously in business. If you want to defuse resistance and encourage collaboration, this is the chapter for you. Following on, Chapter 7 will support this communication section with understanding how to use feelings to truly get to grips with how people are operating and how everyone can benefit when we consider each person properly.

And now the ultimate goal – influencing people with integrity. To be influential is something that many in business wish to attain. Influencing is not to be confused with manipulation. Truly great influential people inspire others to think creatively and come up with high-level ideas. They will be generous in attributing the source of great work and are talented in collaborative innovation that everyone is committed to implementing. If you want to be a great influencer with a talent for engaging people well, ensuring trust and loyalty, you will thoroughly enjoy Chapter 8.

If you understand one thing from this book, it is that the brain is the boss. When we understand a little about the interactions of neurochemicals, hormones and the body, we dissolve mystery. This knowledge empowers us to manage our own behaviour, to understand why we do quirky things, to work out challenges and to keep our superb biological mechanism working well.

It all boils down to influencing oneself and others through integrity by understanding and harnessing emotions at work.

Whatever stage you are at in your career, *Your Brain is Boss* will help you without compromising your health and wellbeing. In fact, following these steps will enhance your emotional, mental, physical and financial wellbeing.

I truly hope you enjoy reading this book and that you find it highly useful.

Let's begin.

Chapter 1
The foundation
**Perception, empathy and
managing conflict**

Chapter 1
The foundation
Perception, empathy and managing conflict

Have you ever heard yourself saying 'I completely understand' or 'I know exactly how you feel'? You know, the type of conversation when someone is confiding in you and you want to show that you are listening and empathise with their situation?

Well, here's the thing, even if you have found yourself in a similar situation to someone else, you will never know exactly how they feel and you will never completely understand. You can't possibly, because there is only perception, and each person's reality will always be different from everyone else's. The complexity of being a human being is quite extraordinary, and each one of us is unique.

This makes it very difficult to understand why people do what they do. And if we don't understand that, how on earth can we respond appropriately and constructively? Equally, do you know how people perceive you? You think you are assertive, but they think you are a bully. You think you are inspiring, but they think you are boring. Do you keep people awake or do you sedate them?

I have a colleague, Steve Houghton-Burnett, who was fascinated by the power of perception when he was leading major change programmes in corporate organisations and the public sector. He noticed that, regardless of the messages being delivered, it was the perception of the people on the receiving end that would mean the difference between a successful project and a failed one.

This chapter is the foundation for you to become an even more influential person than you are now. If you understand exactly how faulty both our perception and memory truly are, you will be in a much better place to understand others and communicate better. It will also help you notice unconscious signals from others so that you can change your behaviour for better results.

Let us begin by discussing that our personal reality is actually an illusion.

What is real? Not a lot.

Two women are pregnant with babies due at exactly the same time. They lovingly call their expectant babies Bump and Wriggler. Both foetuses develop taste buds and begin sampling different flavours as they swallow amniotic fluid in the womb. One mother loves eating cooking apples. Bump tastes the sour taste. After a while the mother starts eating chocolate. Bump tastes the sweetness of the chocolate and shudders because he was used to the sour taste of cooking apples. He doesn't care for the new sweet taste very much. On the other hand, Wriggler's mother loves chocolate, so Wriggler is used to tasting sweet. Wriggler's mother tries some of her friend's cooking apple. Wriggler shudders at the sour taste of the cooking apple. Wriggler doesn't care for this new sour taste very much.

The women share a bowl of olives. Bump and Wriggler react to the salty taste differently because of their experiences so far. Perception is born way before they are. Gradually, while still in the womb, they are introduced to more sensations, layer upon layer, with each new experience being evaluated dependent upon the mix of experiences before. A massively complex pyramid of perceptions has begun.

You may be thinking, 'Oh no! Bump is going to live a life without chocolate.' Never fear, nothing is set in stone.

You see, it all begins very early in pregnancy when taste buds start to develop where the tongue will grow. Even in the first trimester, neurons will have connected with these developing taste buds. But in order to taste, the baby needs taste pores, which develop on the surface of the tongue during the second trimester. It is around this time that the baby will be swallowing amniotic fluid and it will be able to taste five basic flavours – sweet, salty, bitter, sour and umami, which is described in Japan as a pleasant savoury taste. Of course, the intensity of the taste will not be as strong as the mother's sense of taste, because she will be using other senses to evaluate full flavours by using smell, texture, the context of eating and drinking and so on.

Therefore, once we are born and growing, all our senses will contribute to the physical manifestation of taste, which is how we develop a more sophisticated palate.

So there is hope for Bump yet, because it is highly likely that his limited taste in food will expand depending on what he becomes exposed to. Nevertheless, you can see how this infinite mathematical equation begins, and it continues throughout our lives. It builds exponentially to a calculation that is way beyond our capabilities to imagine. No wonder our perceptions are unique to only us.

Perception is an individual dynamic.

If you would like to read more about early development of human flavour preferences read the work of Mennella and Beauchamp (1996).

What has memory got to do with perception?

There is more to consider about our perceived reality. Our unique perceptions are encoded in our memory. This in itself creates more ambiguity. For instance, American neuroscientist Christof Koch has shown that what we tend to see is just the gist of a place or event, especially when we are not giving something our full attention (Koch, 2004). To recall that memory, we have to fill in the gaps based on our previous experiences and perceptions. In psychology this is known as scripts and schemas. Clearly this is not a perfect system.

We only see the 'gist' and fill in the rest.

An example of this comes from the original research of Herman von Helmholtz, a major contributor to physics, physiology and psychology. He developed a theory of visual perception that proposed that, because of the inadequate information provided by the senses, perception cannot be directly derived from the stimulus input alone: to derive meaning, a constructive process is needed to mediate between our sensory information and our conscious perception of the external world (from our store of learnt information). He hypothesised that in order to construct percepts, one draws on 'unconscious inferences'; for instance, our expectations or experiences tell us that a house has four walls, therefore we see a house even when only one wall is in view (von Helmholtz, cited in Gordon, 1989).

And there is more. To add to the complexities of perception, we may confuse another's experience with our own. For instance, children adopt a memory of a sibling as if it were their own. This is not wilful, it's normal.

We confuse others' experiences with our own.

And there is even more. When we recall an event, we inadvertently leave something out or even add a little more information. Memories of past experiences are known as episodic or autobiographical memories and are susceptible to variation at point of recall because our sense of self, who we are at that moment, is constantly changing. Therefore, recalling a memory is dependent upon our environment at the moment of recall.

Again this is not wilfully trying to manipulate the so-called 'truth', but it does lead to distorted memories.

> **Each time we recall a memory we change it slightly.**

Memory is a vast topic, but these simple observations serve to demonstrate that our new experiences are perceived according to our massive equation of past perceptions and put in the mix of remembered experiences. So our perceptions are rendered as even more unique. We cannot say they are wrong because we have no way of knowing what is right. Reality is purely an individual dynamic.

> **Memory is not to be relied upon.**

Why is this important in business? It's actually important to everyone, both inside and outside of business life. So often we do not hear or see accurately what someone is trying to communicate, because we get the gist and fill in the gaps according to our own experience and perception so far. This new perception of the conversation or event can easily be inaccurate because, to a certain extent, we process what we expect, not what is offered.

By default, reality is a personal illusion; there is only individual perception.

Considering all of this, next time someone is telling you about a difficult challenge they are going through, please refrain from saying 'I completely understand' or 'I know exactly how you feel' because, quite frankly, you don't. Even if you have gone through something almost identical, how you feel, how you perceive the situation, how you respond, etc., will be totally different from how the other person is experiencing it. Knowing what perception truly means is the foundation of great communication. If we want to understand what someone is saying we need to concentrate with all our attention using all sensory cues, otherwise little will change because we will fumble along seeing things our own way, which is notoriously unreliable.

So what do you say? How can you communicate well? How can you be a great listener in order to build a clear two-way exchange of understanding?

Does empathy really work?

In order to gain a level of understanding about another person, we need to try to work out how they are feeling in a particular situation. What is it like from their perspective? How might they be thinking? How do they feel? This is empathy.

It is thought that we have developed empathy to gain an understanding of others. Think of crying at a sad film. When we cry at someone else's misfortune, our tears and sadness help us gain a better understanding of what they are going through.

Emotional empathy

Empathy is a key skill in helping you understand what people are feeling and thinking. When you use empathy, you can even recognise emotional states without any words being spoken. It's as if their emotions are contagious. This is highly useful if you are working with people from different social and cultural backgrounds. It may be subjective, but it helps us to connect with people and build strong relationships. And this helps us influence outcomes in all sorts of areas, including understanding better what the customer needs so that we can sell products that suit them, target marketing projects more accurately, and motivate staff to ensure solid employee engagement and lower attrition rates.

> **Emotional empathy transcends the spoken word, but be careful.**

There is a caveat, however. If you continually use emotional empathy in this way it can be exhausting. This is the first moment to consider how to protect yourself but still be an empathetic colleague, supplier and manager. There will be plenty of opportunities in the following chapters to reflect how you can avoid burnout while your business goes from strength to strength. But for the moment, let's consider how a different kind of empathy is sometimes useful.

Being drawn into someone else's emotional world by trying to feel how they feel can sometimes be counterproductive, and when this happens, it's a good idea to stay emotionally detached without tipping into indifference. It would be useless, for instance, if a doctor were to cry with his or her patient. It would be worthless if a lawyer felt the pain of their client. And during an acquisition in business, how could you negotiate if you were too drawn into their emotional world while at the same time trying to deliver redundancy news.

Cognitive empathy

This is not an argument against empathy, however; it's an argument for the merits of a different kind of empathy, which Gerace and colleagues refer to as cognitive empathy (Gerace *et al.*, 2013). This means empathy using the higher-order skills of cognition in the frontal cortex of your brain by imagining what it's like to be that person, rather than using the brain's emotion areas to process how that person is feeling.

Have you ever thought what it's like to actually *be* another person – perhaps a work colleague, your best friend or your life partner? Have you seen what makes them anxious or stressed or even happy? Observing these things will allow you to feel more cognitive empathy for them and to gain a better understanding to pave the way for smoother communication. A connection like this can lead to trust, affiliation and better working relationships without you becoming emotionally exhausted. It can even lower stress, defuse potentially volatile situations and is also an excellent skill to use in negotiations.

To achieve this, you have to use your imagination, you need to imagine what is going on in the other person's mind. What better way to motivate people around you?

Cognitive empathy facilitates understanding.

Compassionate empathy

If you take empathy one step further and feel compelled to help someone, you will be practising compassionate empathy. A fine skill if you are in the caring professions.

Compassionate empathy works when you want to help.

There is a time and place for all three shades of empathy and each can be developed by using imagination, paying attention and observation.

Understand how you come across

I hope the scene is set and you now have a greater understanding about the fragility of perception and memory. Nevertheless, we actually do remarkably well under the circumstances. In addition, I hope you are now comfortable with the idea of using empathy, which offers the greatest opportunity to understand and communicate with people with or without words, and how best to do that depending on various situations.

But this all sounds rather convenient, doesn't it? What about those situations that have already gone sour? What if you find yourself being perceived as someone you are not? Perhaps you try hard to accommodate people and use the skills already mentioned, but somehow people perceive you as weak and seem to have little respect for you.

People often perceive you as being something you are not.

Those people might be highly influential in your career and business activities, and may include people who work for you, your boss, shareholders, customers or clients. One of the core messages in *Your Brain is Boss* is to use emotion for business and personal growth, but not to the extreme of being a push-over that people disrespect and ignore.

How we think we come across is often inaccurate, and we can be oblivious to what and why others may think unfavourably about us. For these very reasons, it's worth being conscious of how others see you in order to ensure understanding, clarity and peace of mind.

Perhaps you could ask for honest, constructive feedback if you have given a presentation or submitted a piece of work. Choose the person you ask for this carefully, and try to pick a sensible, level-headed colleague who is empathetic and progressive. How you respond to that feedback is up to you, but remember you have invited their input and the last thing you should do is get defensive; that will reinforce any negative thoughts about you. So it's a good idea to take feedback with grace, thank the person and go away and think about it. You may find it useful or you may not, but you will have opened up your thinking to evaluate a different perspective from your own.

Constructive feedback can help you understand how others perceive you.

If, after giving things some thought, you realise your intentions were misinterpreted, the best thing to do is apologise. Make an effort to be seen as the person you know you are, and do it a lot. Be consistent in your efforts and gradually people's misguided perceptions of you will change for the better.

Equally, finding things you have in common with people always helps their perceptions of us. What hobbies do you have? Where were you brought up? Even if it's your love of eating crisp sandwiches, you may find others like the same, and you will unconsciously become part of a tribe that will allow people to relate to you better. I'm not suggesting you create groups in a divisive 'them and us' way. But I am suggesting you find common ground with all sorts of people for all sorts of reasons.

Needless to say, great communication is a must, but we can fall down over the simplest things.

Imagine, for instance, a time when you have felt intimidated or are having one of those 'I'm not good enough' days. Let's say you are 13 years old and you have messed up at school in a big way. You are called to the head teacher's office to face the consequences. You approach the office door and any veneer you have carefully created melts unceremoniously as you look at the plaque with large black letters: 'Head's Office – Knock and Wait'.

You knock on the door but, horror of horrors, your meek knock was too quiet to be heard. So you have to go through the agony of knocking again, this time a little louder, but with even shakier hands.

'Come in.'

As you step into the office you are in a worse state than you intended and the Head can sense your fear.

Just the simple meek knock exacerbated the consequences and made the meeting even more painful than it needed to be.

Metaphorically, this happens all the time in business. Walking into a meeting, talking to a colleague, addressing an audience, or even answering the phone, to establish a strong presence, you need to project an authoritative voice. Engagement is crucial. Standing tall, making steady direct eye contact and using pauses to position yourself as thoughtful and confident are all tools a great communicator and a person of influence uses.

These are also excellent negotiation tools. Negotiating starts by listening properly. Your colleagues and teams might have some great ideas which could strengthen a project or the business as a whole. If they have a good idea, tell them, reward their ideas and never take credit for their work. This will improve their self-confidence and they will be grateful to you for the recognition.

What happens when communication goes wrong

Nevertheless, sometimes things still go wrong.

There is often conflict at work because we make the wrong assumptions about the mental state of other people. Sometimes we don't listen properly and don't take into account clues such as face and body language, especially if we use email and social media too much instead of talking. Remember, what we don't know we make up, so if we don't find out what the other person is really thinking, we will assume. They in turn respond to those assumptions with more of their own assumptions, and you get this ghastly yo-yo effect of misunderstandings bouncing back and forth.

> **When misunderstanding meets misunderstanding everything goes wrong.**

This is a recipe guaranteed to misguide perceptions and lead to unnecessary conflict.

I was speaking with corporate peacemaker and mediation expert Jane Gunn (imimediation.org/jane-gunn) and asked what, in her experience, is the negative effect of poor communication and how does this give rise to conflict and even more venom?

This is what she said:

> Most of the problems we encounter in our day-to-day life, whether at home or at work, are with other people and sometimes other people encounter problems with us. Do they tell you? Do you tell them?

> Good and bad points in a relationship are often hidden behind a mask or veneer of sociability. But if you walk around with a mask on and don't share what's really important to you 'How are you?' 'Fine' – 'What's wrong?' 'Nothing', the problem is likely to escalate rather than resolve. And this is so often the case because our instinctive reaction to conflict is to see it as a threat and so it escalates with each person gathering support and advice, determined to 'win' and to destroy the other person rather than listen to, acknowledge and work on solving the problem.

> While children find it easy to be frank with each other, as adults we rarely find it straightforward to talk about our concerns with each other, because the consequences of saying the wrong thing are so much more complex. We might hurt a friendship or lose a job if we say the wrong thing.

If you are constantly worried about avoiding conflict and frequently acquiesce, the likelihood is people will think you are weak rather than a decent person trying to get along with everyone and endeavouring to do a great job. Clearly Jane's message is: ask, listen carefully and keep in mind your aim of collaboration in order to reach a sustainable solution.

Ask and wait for the answer. If you are not satisfied ask again until you reach mutual understanding.

When people perceive you incorrectly it's often because you didn't give them enough information. When you assume they already know something, when you assume they are not interested, when you assume the information might be received unfavourably, things begin to fester. If you fail to relay your messages with clarity it is likely that people will perceive you incorrectly. It is up to you to change this.

Subconscious signals

To be responsible for how we come across to someone else takes vigilance. You have to watch for clues. Does the person look uneasy? Did you see a fleeting expression that is out of context with the conversation? Have they actually done what you asked or perhaps only did just enough to keep you off their backs?

One of the problems is that most of our behaviour is below our level of conscious awareness. Most of the time we don't even know how we have said things or acted.

Think of a time when perhaps you found yourself in a situation where you were desperate for business. If this has happened to you, did you notice how people seemed to magically sense your anxiety and the opportunity passed without a deal being closed? How does that happen?

Or when things are going wrong and people's body language is closed, arms crossed with a furrowed brow, and you haven't even said anything? It's as if people are reading your mind. But they're not, there is no magic.

There is no magic, but there is subconscious signalling.

It is likely that you have subconsciously signalled your anxiety, a sort of subliminal neediness, a begging for business. People buy from successful people and they want a bit of that success.

So if you were perceived as unsuccessful, they will probably avoid you and turn to someone else who they perceive as more successful and do business with them.

So what are those subliminal signals? Dr Paul Ekman has spent his life's work researching facial expressions that convey emotion. He has shown time and time again that people can discriminate between seven classes of facial expression: fear, anger, surprise, happiness, sadness, disgust and contempt (Ekman, 2016). This ability is said to transcend cultural and linguistic barriers, and these facial expressions are not culturally specific, even when taking into account the differing social norms of emotional responses. This is excellent news when trading in our global economy, so definitely worth considering in business.

What is even more useful is Ekman's research into micro-expressions or 'leakage'. These are fleeting glimmers in the eyes of an emotion that the person is either unaware of or they are actively suppressing. When you are aware of what to look for, micro-expressions help you to read an emotional response of a colleague or customer. Of course, we never know what someone else is thinking, so their micro-expression of anger may not be about you but rather a sudden thought about an incident that happened earlier. However, Ekman proposes that these tiny expressions help us to evaluate an emotional state of a person so that we have a chance of predicting their reaction to what we have said and responding appropriately for smoother communication and understanding.

For instance, if you are telling someone they have been made redundant from their job and you notice a fleeting micro-expression that tells you their initial reaction is one of anger, you can react in one of several ways. You can ignore the expression and hope their anger doesn't escalate and make the meeting even harder. You can acknowledge how they may be feeling by saying 'This may not be good news for you, but the business has changed and your talents are no longer the best fit.' Of course, they may still be angry, but at least they know that you have understood how they may be feeling and you have a chance to conduct a sensible conversation. If, however, they go on to full-blown anger it is probably better to say nothing until they have let off some steam.

If you would like to learn more about Ekman's micro-expression training tools, go to his website (paulekman.com). I have studied them myself and you won't be disappointed.

> **Ekman's seven emotional facial expressions are universal therefore worth knowing in business.**

Showing emotion this way doesn't equate to weakness or vulnerability, it equates to an effective reciprocal interaction that transcends ambiguity and facilitates understanding, but you have to be vigilant.

Paying attention and observation

To take control of how you are perceived and how your perception of others can become more accurate, you will need to pay attention and see what's going on around you. This is harder than you think. To prevent information overload from the immeasurable onslaught of sensory information, our brain has limited capacity to attend to every detail. The main purpose of attentional processing, therefore, is to choose particular information for further processing and, in so doing, ignore other information.

We sometimes get this wrong. This is because there is a profusion of stimuli competing for attentional resources at any one time, and selective processing of the significance of what is in front of us is difficult. However, processing the emotional significance of something is said to have an evolutionary advantage in that positive and negative emotion modulates appetitive and defensive behaviour, ultimately leading to reproduction and survival. As such, only a fleeting glimpse of an emotionally relevant cue is sufficient to reach awareness and perception.

Attention is what brings stimuli into our conscious awareness. Perception of emotion, however, can also take place automatically in the absence of attention, that is, below conscious awareness. This view is supported by my own research and the research of many others.

Attention isn't easy but it pays off.

So although you can mindfully give someone your full attention and bring signals to your conscious awareness, you can also detect perceived emotion below conscious awareness that will enhance all communication.

This takes practice and confidence. In summary, perception is the foundation of our own reality, it can make or break understanding. Empathy, vigilance and the following action steps can elevate you into a seat of power and control so that *your brain* becomes a better *boss*.

It's now time to move on to building greater and resilience in the next chapter.

Action steps

1. When you are next in an internal meeting that you regularly attend, start with a lesson in perception. Choose a famous person that everyone knows. Ask everyone to write down what they think of that person – what are they like, how they feel about them. Then get each person to read out what they have written and discuss differences and how the same person was perceived in different ways. This will demonstrate that the perceived differences are not wrong, they are just different.

2. As a team exercise or individually, write down different situations where empathy would give better results. Then add which kind of empathy would work best – emotional, cognitive or compassionate.

3. To work out how people perceive you, ask someone sensible you trust for feedback for a piece of work or the way you handled a situation. Try not to react, but take the information with gratitude and think about it.

4. If you want to change the way people see you, become the person you want them to see. It may not be as obvious as you think. But make sure your favoured behaviour is consistent.

5. Join in. Do things with others. Remember, people make up what they don't know, so make sure they know the positive side of your personality.

6. Make a habit of noticing people's reaction to things. If you sense something is wrong get it out in the open and, if relevant and necessary, apologise.

7. People love to feel good about themselves, so if you want to be perceived favourably, ask for their opinion or advice on something. But be genuine; they will know if you are just trying to glean their favour.

8. If there is conflict, remember it's not right, it's not wrong, it just is. Try not to take other people's responses as a personal threat. They are an alarm for not having enough information. Get the issue out in the open, discuss it from all angles, including ones you hadn't thought of before by asking how they see things. Getting their point of view is more valuable information, and offering your perspective should add to the information pot.

9. If point 8 doesn't yield a respectful resolution, tell the story of Bump and Wriggler. When everyone understands, perception, resolution, collaboration and communication are easier.

10. Step back and observe yourself. Try to feel whatever is going on but don't get involved in the emotion. Look at yourself as if you were an outsider. See how you perceive a situation. Be impartial. This is a great exercise to do any time of the day to get things in perspective.

Chapter 2
Getting fit for the job
Stress busting, resilience training
and managing your time well

Chapter 2
Getting fit for the job
Stress busting, resilience training and managing your time well

The world of work is changing ever more rapidly and we all have to keep up. Mergers and acquisitions constantly change our daily landscape and invariably lead to a shrink in head-counts. Technical innovations, competition on a global scale, new products and information are coming at us from all angles.

It is becoming more commonplace for people to work a portfolio of short-term contracts, part-time employment and entrepreneurial activities. This means we are being forced to spend some of our time marketing ourselves and using social media to further our prospects. If we are not producing work, we are marketing, networking, filling in tax returns and all sorts of other work-related activities, just to keep our heads above water. Even 'permanent' full-time work is no longer guaranteed to be long term. So we are often walking around like two-legged pressure cookers waiting to explode. The good news, however, is that our brains are superb at handling an enormous amount of new data and we are perfectly able to keep up, but only if we look after this magnificent biological lump of matter inside us, our brain, and don't take it for granted. Your brain is boss, and like all other bosses, it needs handling wisely so that you can become more influential at work.

This chapter is intended to help you realise your ambitions without burning out. It is aimed at providing you with knowledge and the skills to handle those curve balls with resilience and good health so that you can enjoy your family and friends and have a good life outside of work, and stay out of the doctor's surgery. If you get a handle on the skills we are about to discuss, you are on the road to greater success, higher self-esteem and fulfilment.

We will start with understanding what stress is and how it can destroy even the best of intentions. To combat stress, we need to build resilience, which is a skill everyone needs in order to survive and thrive, and we can develop it by working on five categories of wellbeing – emotional, career, physical, financial and mental. The final section of this chapter looks at a problem people from all sectors in business and the professions seem to have – how to manage time well to avoid feeling overwhelmed. When we are on top of managing our precious time, we have a huge advantage in making progress.

First then, let's look at one of our greatest enemies if we let it get out of control. Stress.

The number one problem today is stress.

Why stress is so toxic

The most insidious, toxic problem each of us has is stress. It is the underpinning of high blood pressure, anxiety disorders, depression, heart disease, addictions, and even some cancers.

Life events can be highly stressful. The major culprits are bereavement, divorce, unemployment and moving house. These huge stressors are dreadful to deal with, but deal with them we do. Gradually over time, things improve and our stress levels diminish. These major events do not have the most toxic effect, however; it is the everyday erosion that doesn't go away which causes health problems. The everyday issues that we can't seem to get on top of, whether it be the computer system that frequently won't do what you need it to for the outcomes you require, the nasty colleague who won't go away, the to-do list that just gets longer. It is steady and repeated issues like these that cause chronic stress and that can, in turn, damage your health and your business.

This is how it works

When we are in a stressful situation (stressor) the brain secretes stress hormones, which are the body's chemical messengers (stress response). Basically, the process is that the brain receives a stressor and this triggers arousal, the consequence of which is the same whether we are frightened or excited (for example, the biologist Sapolsky (1994) offers the example of a lion chasing a zebra, which elicits the same stress response in both animals). Once arousal has been triggered, we either secrete the hormone epinephrine (similar to the neurotransmitter noradrenaline) for a fast response to make us run or get ready to compete, or the cortisol pathway is activated more slowly and does many things, such as turning off some areas of our bodily systems that are not immediately needed to deal with the stressful situation. You can therefore appreciate why a consequence of stress responses is the compromising of our immunity system, meaning that in stressful periods we are more likely to fall victim to ailments such as colds and flu or to experience digestive problems.

Now don't get me wrong, exposure to cortisol in small amounts is actually good for us; it helps us survive, it keeps us on our toes and helps us stay alert, it arouses us to get the job done. Chronic stress, however, is far more extreme, and when cortisol levels remain elevated for a long time, it compromises more than our immunity system. We may also experience memory loss because the hippocampus area of the brain (associated with memory) contains a high density of cortisol receptors and can be compromised when exposed to prolonged cortisol levels. An added problem is that it's the job of the hippocampus to detect cortisol in the blood and message the hypothalamus to reduce blood-cortisol levels. But if the hippocampus is damaged, the messages are not sent, resulting in prolonged exposure to cortisol. This is greatly damaging to our wellbeing and can also lead to high blood pressure and related problems.

Cortisol has a strong relationship with the feel-good neurotransmitters secreted by the brain, such as serotonin. Just as with cortisol, we need just the right amount of serotonin in our system to sleep well, eat properly and to regulate our mood and emotions. Chronic exposure to cortisol results in an imbalance which can lead to depression and the regular prescription of antidepressant drugs known as selective serotonin reuptake inhibitors (SSRIs), which are intended to restore the chemical balance by increasing the amount of serotonin and norepinephrine.

Another neurotransmitter stimulated by cortisol is dopamine, a chemical working along the popularly named pleasure pathway in the brain, targeting areas controlling reward and motivation.

Through these observations you can see how stress can cause havoc in the brain and body. It can have a devastating effect on your work and home life. So let's see what we can do about it.

How stressed are you right now?

With the above science overview in mind, ask yourself these questions:

- Do you find difficulty in communicating with your colleagues and family?
- Are there misunderstandings?
- Do you explode or fester in a corner at something someone says?
- Do you frequently feel angry or frustrated in your work?
- Are you sleeping poorly?
- Do you constantly feel tired?
- Do you overeat or not eat enough?
- Do you need that first cup of coffee in the morning to function?
- Do you suffer from frequent headaches or digestive problems?
- Are you on any prescribed drugs for stress-related problems?

Is there anything in this list to which you can honestly say 'Yes, that's me'? How many do you relate to – one, two, three or more? Remember, this isn't an exhaustive list. Perhaps you can think of something you are suffering with that is not listed here but that you believe is exacerbated by stress?

These questions are worth asking yourself every now and again. As life moves on, circumstances change and stress levels vary constantly. The trick is how to build resilience to cope with this ever-changing landscape. In each of the following subsections you will find a how-to list, so be ready to make some positive changes in your life.

> **Life is full of curve balls, learn to dodge them, deal with them and bounce back.**

Resilience and wellbeing

Being fit to cope with the curve balls in life means that you can not only dodge them with ease but you can also deal with them if they land in your back yard and you will bounce back quickly. This is resilience. To be fit enough to be resilient we all need to look after our wellbeing. To truly get to grips with wellbeing it is useful to break it down into five areas:

> **Optimum resilience means looking after all areas of wellbeing.**

1. Emotional wellbeing – social and community wellbeing
2. Career wellbeing
3. Physical wellbeing
4. Financial wellbeing
5. Mental wellbeing

Exercise to assess how you are doing in the five categories of wellbeing

Consider each of the five areas, one at a time:

Emotional wellbeing – ask yourself if you recover quickly from setbacks and are able to understand the strengths of emotions so that you can move forward and progress in a positive direction.

Career wellbeing – when you wake up in the morning do you look forward to your day, do you like what you do and feel valuable?

Physical wellbeing – how are your energy levels, do you feel healthy even within the restrictions of a chronic condition? In other words, are you as healthy as you can be to do what you want to do?

Financial wellbeing – are you effective at managing your bank balance?

Mental wellbeing – how are your levels of stress or anxiety?

On a scale of 1–10 (1 is extremely badly, 10 is extremely well), how do you score in each of the areas?

Write your answers on a piece of paper. Add them up and divide the total by 5.

If you scored more than 7, congratulations, you are doing very well. A score of 4–6 means you are struggling some-what, while 3 or less is an indication that you are probably suffering, and if this continues, the chances are that you may be at risk of becoming unwell.

Whatever your score, you can improve it by reading this next section.

Let's briefly look at each of the five areas of wellbeing.

Learn to be in control of your emotions rather than emotions controlling you.

Emotional wellbeing is your ability to understand the value of your emotions and being able to control them, rather than emotions controlling you. It is being able to use emotion to function well when things go wrong. Emotional wellbeing enables you to realise your strengths, to feel good about yourself with a healthy level of self-worth and self-esteem. And it helps you to identify what makes you happy and to be proactive in making positive changes with focus and energy. Of course, this doesn't mean arrogance or being egocentric. There is a fine balance, and humility helps with that balance.

Strong relationships are fundamental to our wellbeing.

As well as the personal level, it has to be recognised that, as a result of our evolution, we are meant to live in a tribe and this is fundamental to our emotional wellbeing too. So social wellbeing requires that we have a strong social network around us, within which we have things in common with other members and we support one another and develop trust. It is about loving people and being loved in return.

Community wellbeing can be considered as reaching out to people with whom we might not have such things in common or such close bonds. Perhaps your neighbours need a helping hand. The effect on our general wellbeing when we help someone without expecting anything in return is detailed in Chapter 8, but suffice to say that exercising altruism, kindness and generosity will help you flourish. Regardless of whether you are religious, spiritual or an atheist, I'm sure you will recognise times when you felt so much better by thinking of others or undertaking acts of kindness. Such actions stop us looking inward and feeling sorry for ourselves but expand our thinking and give us respite from our own problems.

Action steps: how to improve emotional wellbeing

1. Read the next chapter in this book on emotional intelligence.
2. Actively keep in touch with people you like – call them, meet for coffee, go for a walk.
3. Develop new relationships by joining a club of some kind that suits you.
4. Ask people questions without prying, be interested in people.
5. Offer to help whenever you can.
6. Make a list of the things you are good at and do those. Forget the rest.
7. Realise that emotion isn't the enemy, it is a barometer to tell you when things aren't right. Listen to the clues.

Emotional wellbeing is not a pink fluffy topic, it's a serious part of our general health and is a solid way to avoid stress-related disorders.

Career wellbeing

Become positively forensic and scrutinise what you love about your work and what you don't.

There are many lucky people out there who love the work they do. They enjoy going to work and they find their job fulfilling and purposeful. To like your job is career wellbeing. And if you are one of these people, *go you*! It's utterly brilliant and long may it last.

On the other hand, there are an enormous number of people who do not like their job, they do not find it satisfying and spend the working week looking forward to time off. Tim Rath and Jim Harter wrote in their book *Wellbeing* (2010) that only 20 per cent of the people they asked truly liked what they did every day. And more importantly, this meant that those who were not happy in their career didn't enjoy their weekends very much either. This indicates that a negative mindset spills over into all areas of your life. This is dreadful news. How awful not to fully enjoy things you used to love doing outside of work.

If you feel stuck in a job you are not enjoying, become a forensic detective and look at every fine detail of your job, both good and bad. Work out what you enjoy and do more of that; and work out what needs changing, then set out to make those changes.

Action steps: how to improve career wellbeing

1. If the job is mundane, try injecting a bit of interest or excitement to make it more entertaining for yourself.
2. If you don't like your colleagues, can you make an effort to go for a coffee with them and get to know them better? You may be surprised to learn what they are really like.
3. How about starting a sports team at lunchtime or after work and getting into a team league?
4. If you seek promotion, are you putting the right steps in place to achieve it (for instance, can your boss or a mentor help you climb the ladder)?
5. Can you go on courses to gain better qualifications to aid that promotion?
6. Do you need a new job? If so, start looking.
7. Go back to your list of what you enjoy doing at work and seek out ways of working this into your day.

Whatever you do, don't dismiss career wellbeing as just 'one of those things' that you can do nothing about and which is not important. It is. It's extremely important.

Physical wellbeing

> **Physical exercise is for the brain and body. Stress busting at its best.**

We all know about this one, don't we? We all know that exercise is good for us. But research shows that there is a direct link between physical activity and brain function. When we exercise, we release 'feel-good' neurotransmitters such as endorphins, but we also release neurochemicals that support the physical structure of the brain and help develop its infrastructure. I have heard people say that the brain is a muscle. It is not. But the brain does grow with activity and shrinks without.

When we exercise, we put ourselves in a better mood, we feel more positive, we sleep better, we achieve respite from our worries as we concentrate on throwing that basketball or lifting those weights. Even if we simply go for a walk, the rhythm is like an active meditation (more about that in the mental wellbeing section).

When it comes to exercise, the secret is to do what you enjoy doing. There is no point in hating an exercise regime, because that's unsustainable and you will give up. Ask yourself what you enjoy doing or what physical activity you enjoyed as a child.

Wherever you are on the fitness scale, the challenge is always finding time for exercise or physical activity in a busy schedule, so it needs to become a routine, a habit that fits in. Perhaps try getting up earlier and exercising first thing in the morning to kick off your day (having gone to bed that little bit earlier the night before!). Or try some regular evenings after work, on your own or with colleagues, or even first thing on a weekend morning before the family is up and about. The choice is yours; you can make it happen.

If you are still a reluctant exerciser, there is an excellent book called *Spark* by Professor John Ratey and Eric Hagerman. Professor Ratey is an associate clinical professor of psychiatry at Harvard Medical School and he says, 'Exercise is… simply one of the best treatments we have for most psychiatric problems' (2009, p.7). Now that's quite a statement.

And if you want any anecdotal evidence, you only need to search on the Internet to read about the habits of successful people and you will find a long list of the great and the good who exercise daily. People like Richard Branson founder of the Virgin Group; Nancy Pelosi, US congresswoman; Michael Corbat, CEO of Citigroup, and many more. The list is endless.

There is no doubt that exercise helps us feel in control of our bodies. This leads to greater confidence, and physical activity raises our mental capacity and lowers stress.

On taking up or stepping up exercise, we must not overlook that as we increase our physical output, it is important to ensure that we have a highly nutritious diet and drink plenty of water. There are many resources that tell you how to eat well. But there is a simple rule I follow – make sure it's a colourful plate, and I don't mean the pattern on the china! Some lean protein (fish, meat, beans, nuts, etc.), complex carbohydrates (brown rice, sweet potatoes) and plenty of a wide range of vegetables and salad. Add some dairy, fruit and seeds if you wish, and your physical wellbeing will be enhanced. By the way, if you have any food intolerances it may be worth seeking professional advice.

Action steps: how to improve physical wellbeing

1. Seek medical advice if you haven't exercised for a while.
2. Assess where you are now. Record your weight and how fit you are.

3. Think about your fitness objectives (e.g. do you want to lose weight by the summer, do you want to enter a marathon, do you want to gain a general level of fitness, do you want to tone up for a special event?).

4. Seek out and create a routine that will get you to your objectives.

5. Make sure you enjoy your plan otherwise you won't stick to it. If you hate running, don't run. Do what you enjoy, as long as it's moving!

6. Turn this into a daily habit and eat well with plenty of water.

7. Vary your activity, but remember, if you take on a heavy training programme give yourself time to recover in between your sessions.

Financial wellbeing

Putting your head in the sand is no way to improve your finances, be proactive.

This is an interesting one and, in my experience, a wellbeing category that many overlook or ignore. They ignore it because they think it's too hard, too depressing or outside of their control.

I spoke with Jeanette Makings, Head of Financial Education at Close Brothers Asset Management, a company working with employers across the UK providing financial education and advice to help improve financial wellbeing for employees throughout their career. I asked Jeanette how she would describe financial wellbeing. Jeanette suggests beginning by understanding where you are now in terms of your personal finances, having an idea of where you would actually like to be with your finances – in other words, what your goals and objectives are – and then finding ways to attain your goals with the financial opportunities that are available to you. But she was keen to emphasise that financial wellbeing is not about making everyone wealthy, but it is about people feeling in control, feeling that that they have a plan and they are more confident about the steps they can take to 'cause positive change' and make the most of their own circumstances. I like that. Jeanette suggested financial wellbeing can be thought of in seven easy steps.

Action steps: how to improve financial wellbeing

1. Planning and budgeting – recognise what you currently have and set out a plan of where you want to go. Take control of your budget, how much you've got coming in and how much you're spending, and really use your budget to help you make changes so you can move towards the things you want to do.

2. Managing debt – it sounds obvious, but work out how much you owe and review whether it would be better to rearrange your debt and set out a plan in your budget which will enable you to take control and better manage your debt or even pay it off altogether and become debt free.

3. Protection – unplanned events (redundancy, ill health and so on) happen. Considering these and protecting against the risks that are most important to you and your family is an important part of your personal financial plans. This will help you feel better and is likely to reduce stress levels.

4. Savings – whether these are for short-term matters such as a holiday or longer-term plans such as for a home or retirement, the most important part of this area of financial planning is to have a plan and to save regularly.

5. Planning for retirement – while for some people this may seem like a long way off, saving enough for what may be 25+ years in retirement takes time, and the sooner you start and the longer you save, the better.

6. Investments – making your hard-earned money work for you and beat inflation.

7. Tax efficiency – no one likes to pay more tax than they need to, so ensuring you understand, for example, that you are on the right tax code and what allowances and reliefs are available for you seems like a very good plan.

All these tips are to point you towards gaining control of your finances. Of course, it is still stressful if you don't have enough money, but at least having all the facts means you will feel much better and be able to work towards improving your financial plan. Knowledge is power when it comes to finances.

Mental wellbeing

> **'Meditation? I can't do it'. Well you won't master it in three days. But you will benefit if you keep practising.**

Mental illness is on the increase and anything we can do to help ourselves can only be good.

All the states of wellbeing we have mentioned so far contribute in part to our mental wellbeing. Now let us look at other areas in which we can make further positive change to our mental wellbeing through resilience and coping mechanisms.

Meditation, mindfulness and sleep. We cannot ignore the benefits of what happens in the brain when we meditate. Yes, I know meditation can be hard. Maybe you've tried previously (for a whole three days!) and decided you couldn't do it. But those who can manage some kind of meditation and benefit from it keep practising, even when their runaway mind would rather think about how many ants there are in the world or what happens if you throw jelly at a window. They keep practising and gradually can spend 5 minutes of meditation time and not be aware of where it went. Now that's what we're talking about. Of course, you may be a seasoned meditator and have this skill nicely tucked away in your kitbag. But if you want to read on and get to grips with working on mental wellbeing let's first look at what brain frequencies mean.

The billions of neurons in our brain communicate with one another in one of two ways: by chemicals or by passing an electrical signal from one neuron to another via a connection called a synapse. For the purposes of this topic, let's just look at the electrical activity.

Electrical signals between neurons work in harmony and create a neural network; this activity is called a brainwave. Brainwaves have different frequencies.

- Gamma waves (25–100 Hz, typically 40 Hz): the fastest pattern of neural oscillations associated with conscious perception.
- Beta waves (12–25 Hz): alert and focused, our normal awake state. Studies show that if we get stuck in this frequency we can become depressed or anxious.
- Alpha waves (8–12 Hz): daydreaming, meditating. Associated with creative thought.
- Theta waves (3–8 Hz): REM sleep and a deep meditation that practised meditators can achieve.
- Delta waves (0.5–3 Hz): the slowest frequency achieved when we are in deep dreamless sleep.

Do you remember when you were at school and the teacher would tell you off for staring out of the window? Admonishments such as 'stop daydreaming and get on with your work' were often said but were foolhardy. According to researchers Rani and Rao (1996), dreaming or slowing brain frequencies down to alpha is one of the most sensible things you can do to improve attention, and Sobolewski and colleagues (2011) show that this will also help you gain greater emotional control and, of course, reduce stress. In further research which studied the effects of meditation on the brain, neuroscientist Sara Lazar at Harvard Medical School found that after people meditated daily for eight weeks, several areas of the brain changed, resulting in an increase in memory, resilience, compassion and empathy (Lazar, 2011).

Recently, what is termed *mindfulness* has grown in popularity. The term means 'to observe whatever you are doing mindfully, without judgement'. Many people find it easier to get into the habit of using mindfulness rather than meditating, as you can employ this anytime, anywhere. One study by Ren and his team showed that 'watchful' meditation had more of a beneficial effect on increasing our ability to solve problems, more so than relaxation methods (Ren *et al.*, 2011).

Many studies support the efficacy of meditation and mindfulness, and further studies continue to examine the effects of specific techniques and their consequent effects on our brain and behaviour. The important thing to remember, however, is that thoughts become clearer when you slow down your brain and, by default, you become more confident and resilient as you become less affected by that which is not important. This approach results in far less stress, and research shows that we can turbocharge our path to success.

While still on the subject of mental wellbeing, one of the biggest threats to our mental stability is lack of sleep, even though we sometimes read reports of people who are highly successful while needing little more than 4 hours sleep a night. There are no universal recommendations about how much sleep each of us needs, but it is clear that the quality of sleep is important in order to heal our bodies, process information and consolidate memories.

It comes as no surprise that sleep deprivation has been used as a form of torture. When we do not sleep well, our immune system is weakened and we may suffer from anxiety and depression. Can you imagine not sleeping at all? The effect can be devastating on our ability to think clearly. If you have problems sleeping, this can have a serious adverse effect on your chances of promotion or any other business success, let alone having a devastating impact on relationships as your tolerance levels plummet to rock bottom.

Here are some ideas that may help you sleep, along with some meditation and mindfulness tips.

Action steps: how to improve mental wellbeing

1. Choose one method of either mindfulness or meditation that suits you.
2. If you are new to this, tenacity is the key. Keep practising.
3. A simple way is to count the breath. For instance, count to 5 on the in-breath and 5 on the out-breath.
4. Start with just 5 minutes twice a day and see if you can build up to 20 minutes twice a day.
5. Keep a log of your progress to monitor the effect. You could even make it a mini experiment and note how you feel today and how you feel after a month of meditation or mindfulness.
6. If your quality of sleep is poor, check that your body is the right temperature in bed. Is it too bright in your room or are there noises that disturb you? Move electronic devices such as laptop computers or mobile phones out of the bedroom. Change what you can and see if it helps.
7. Think about what you do just before trying to go to sleep. Do you eat late, not drink enough water, keep a computer on until lights out? All of these things can disturb your sleep pattern.

> **'I have so much to do today, I'm going to have to meditate twice as long.' – Gandhi.**

There are plenty of computer or mobile phone applications these days that are easy to listen to for guided meditation, or provide lessons in mindfulness and relaxation techniques to help you sleep. Thinking you don't have time is not true.

If you want to grow your business properly or climb the corporate ladder, you will need to cover the basics in wellbeing first. To do all of the things suggested here may be too much, but you will make a positive change if you adopt just one action from each section of wellbeing. Develop a skill set that is the foundation to kick-start or supercharge a highly successful career, no matter how long you have been working.

There is one other enormous stressor that seems to affect most people and that is managing one's time without feeling overwhelmed. Let's now see if you can improve this and add it to your skill set once and for all.

Managing your time

> **Time management is an illusion. It's 'overwhelm' we need to tackle.**

I have been asked many times to work with senior executives to improve their time-management strategies. It seems that regardless of profession or type of industry, many people feel the need to address their time-management skills as they are constantly drowning in workload.

We can all relate to an ever-increasing workload, but forgive me when I say that each time I stand in front of top business leaders, lawyers, accountants and so on to deliver time-management workshops, I wonder what on earth I am doing there. I look out at a sea of faces and I invariably see a group of highly intelligent, resourceful, focused individuals who have proven themselves on numerous occasions in terms of time management. If they hadn't, they wouldn't be such high achievers. People don't otherwise accumulate academic achievements, an abundance of skills, business success or lucrative lifestyles. Frankly, I have sometimes felt almost a fraud by extolling the virtues of time management when clearly the delegates have previously proven themselves in this field tenfold.

I have pondered this dilemma for some time and this is what I think is happening. To a certain extent, the overriding problem is being overwhelmed by incomplete tasks. This is partly due to our constant internal chatter:

- 'I know I'm going to be *found out*. They will work out I don't know what I'm doing if I ask a question.'
- 'I'm not going to ask for help, I will just look stupid.'
- 'I'm not going to delegate, no one does the job as well as me.'
- 'I'm just going to go over this piece of work one more time. It needs to be perfect.'
- 'I'm frightened of losing control, please don't let anyone notice.'

This isn't a time-management problem, it's a fear problem. Most of us know and use various time-management techniques, from dedicated task lists to delegation, but in truth, how much time do we truly spend on 100 per cent uninterrupted focused work?

The latter point is huge. Interruptions, false starts and procrastination cloud our perception of how much time we actually spend productively. We tend to compound this with unrealistic ideas as to how long a task or project could take.

Feeling overwhelmed or out of control is such a stressful way to start our working day. As soon as the brain secretes more of the stress hormone cortisol than is useful, we are wired to narrow down our focus to concentrate on the perceived threat for survival. The side effect of this is that we can no longer think broadly about our work, and crucially we can no longer think creatively to do the job well.

With this in mind, I recall a book I used to read to my children at bedtime. It was a beautiful book called *Starbright* by Maureen Garth, which had a different story in each chapter, though each chapter began the same way. The stories always began with the child approaching a 'worry tree' where they would be encouraged to pin all their worries on the trunk of the tree. Once this task was complete, they would open a door and enter the tree. Once inside, a whole host of magical journeys lay in front of them to choose, such as floating on clouds or rocking gently in boats. Naturally, the child would drift into a worry-free sleep.

We all loved this book, so why can't we do this as adults? I don't suggest you enter a tree and go off on a magical journey at the start of your working day (or perhaps that's not such a bad idea!), but the worry tree concept is a splendid idea. Dumping concerns on sticky pieces of paper can help clear your head to get on with the tasks that need to be done. Or, of course, you could use some of your wellbeing skills such as physical exercise first thing, followed by a few minutes of meditation to clear your head and focus clearly. You can always go back to the concerns once you have achieved a few goals.

Aligning with this way of thinking is a powerful way to manage your diary. Many associates of mine insist on putting their vacations into the diary before anything else. Along with time to spend with family and friends, block out some time for exercise, hobbies and fun and anything else that is going to help your physical, mental and emotional wellbeing.

Once the leisure pursuits are in place, it's amazing how you can realistically see what time is left to get the real work done. It seems to galvanise people into focusing and just getting on with it, firm in the knowledge that playtime is just around the corner. A perfect set-up for the brain to produce a cocktail of 'feel-good' neurotransmitters to make us even more efficient.

In this context, shrinking fear by parking worries and prioritising pleasant pursuits is a far more productive way of working efficiently. Time management is not so elusive after all, is it?

> ## Perfectionism is not necessarily something to be proud of.

Do you consider yourself to be a perfectionist? If so, are you proud to announce this to the world, like wearing perfectionism as a badge of honour, an accolade that translates as a hard-working, thorough contributor to the workforce?

Here's the news. Perfectionism is not something to be proud of. It can even become an illness, a risk factor for compulsive personality disorder.

Perfectionism is referenced in the Diagnostic and Statistical Manual of Mental Disorders (DSM), which is a classification and diagnostic manual used universally for psychiatric diagnoses. At the moment, we are on the fifth edition (DSM-5). On page 242 it states that 'Obsessive-compulsive personality disorder... involves an enduring and pervasive maladaptive pattern of excessive perfectionism and rigid control'. It also states on page 678 that the obsessive-compulsive personality 'shows perfectionism that interferes with task completion (e.g. is unable to complete a project because his or her own overly strict standards are not met). Is excessively devoted to work and productivity to the exclusion of leisure activities and friendships (not accounted for by obvious economic necessity).'

I think the point about 'interfering with task completion' is highly relevant in a business environment. Not getting work out on time for fear of it not being perfect is damaging to business and reputations.

Before you go away thinking your perfectionism is the worst thing, bear this in mind. If you have high standards, but you are happy to send work out when necessary even when it's not perfect, your perfectionism is normal and healthy. In fact, the chances are you are a high achiever. The point of mentioning some of the criteria for perfectionism as a personality disorder is to ask you to be careful. It's a good idea to check in with yourself now and again and make sure you have things in perspective. If you haven't, try taking some time out and relax a little.

Delegation

> **Delegation is a skill that can be learnt. If you don't learn it, you will probably burn out.**

It's hard to delegate, isn't it? To trust other people to get the job done. The problem is, the more senior we become, the more we have to delegate because we simply can't do everything personally. Ambitious people must delegate, and delegate well, otherwise it's totally counterproductive in terms of stress, wellbeing and productivity.

The first step is to decide what someone else can do. To a certain extent, you have to trust them, but you can put some steps in place to help them grow into the task and do it well.

For instance, how good are you at explaining what needs to be done? Do you offer the whole picture or do you just ask them to do a small part of the overall job? In my experience, the former helps people to see where they fit in and why the job is so important, and it also helps them feel an important part of the process or project. So, aim to give the whole story and explain each component of the task, even if it's only photocopying. For instance, if the person you are delegating to knows that an important client needs these documents by 9 am tomorrow morning because they will be deciding which firm gets the work, they are far more likely to do the job efficiently and effectively.

While you are explaining what needs to be done make sure the person has all the resources they need and that your instructions are clear, and let them know they can ask you if they are not sure. You will be surprised how often I hear that intelligent people hide in their office, stuck and not doing anything productive because they are worried about asking again. This shouldn't happen.

Once you have explained clearly, let them get on with it. Don't micromanage; that is soul destroying and disrespectful. But do monitor how things are going.

And when the job is done, it's feedback time. Here, the best thing you can say is 'How do you think that went?' After all, they are the ones who know better than you because they did the work and they will be able to tell you exactly how it went, what went well, what went wrong. In effect, they will be giving themselves the feedback and you will learn so much more.

A good delegator nurtures relationships of trust and respect. People do things well when we just take the time to do things properly to start with. And think how much more you can achieve when you have trusted people who can help you.

Circadian rhythms and working

Being a lark or an owl can make a difference to your working day.

While considering how to manage our time better it's worth mentioning our internal biological rhythms, or circadian rhythms, the day and night rhythms that are central to our sleep–wake cycle.

Consider your own circadian rhythm for efficiency at work. It is generally recognised that at the beginning of the working day we are not fully alert, so this could be a good time to catch up on emails and less important tasks. We become fully alert approaching lunchtime, which is the ideal time to have a major impact on tasks that require our full attention. Once we have eaten lunch our energy drops (and this isn't just to do with eating lunch, this is part of the rhythm), so getting back to social media and emails may be a fit. Gradually as the afternoon progresses, we become more alert and can get back to tasks requiring fuller attention, although it is at this time that we are susceptible to distractions. When the early evening arrives and we are beginning to feel tired is when we can settle into thinking about something that requires a bit more creative thought.

Of course, if you are a 'lark' you may have to adjust these times to slightly earlier. And conversely, if you are an 'owl' adjust the times to an hour later. Equally, this may be too prescriptive for you, especially if you spend most of your day in meetings. If this is the case, try noticing your own energies, when do you feel most alert? Take note over a few days and arrange your workload accordingly.

This is useful to keep in mind if you wish to work with your biological clock for peak performance. It becomes tricky, however, if you wish for a team of people (who are probably a mix of larks and owls) to enjoy the same advantages, as it's likely their circadian rhythms will be slightly different. Nevertheless, experimenting for a while by designating tasks to match circadian rhythms may yield excellent results.

For good measure, here is a list of tips to help with better use of your time. Some you will know and some perhaps not, but all are useful reminders.

Action steps: how to use your time well

1. Prioritise with two to-do lists, one for work and one for your personal life. Forgetting a birthday card can impact on your stress levels, so all tasks are important. Pick the most important three or four for the day in each list and get those done first.
2. See your friends and family; they will be your anchor and ground you.

3. Delegate where you can, at home and at work. But remember to give a thorough briefing and make sure they have all the tools and knowledge they need. Follow up to see how they got on. Ask them how they think it went.

4. Be realistic about how long things can take. There is no point in putting yourself under more pressure because you underestimated timings for completion.

5. Handle paper only once. Action it, file it or bin it. Don't pile it.

6. Create the perfect filing system that is simple so that others can help you.

7. When calling someone on the phone and talking to their voicemail, leave a message with details of when you can be reached, to avoid playing telephone ping-pong.

8. When making phone calls, have a notebook to hand with a brief agenda of what you want to achieve with the call and make further notes/actions while speaking to the person.

9. Leave alarms and messages to remind you of your schedule.

10. Don't procrastinate, prioritise and just get on with it.

11. Clutter distracts and it's hard to find things quickly. It also causes anxiety. Tidying up helps you stay calm.

12. Achieved a deadline? Excellent. Reward yourself with a bit of down time, even if it's going for a walk around the block.

13. Notebooks – if you use one, try using the front for your to-do lists and the back for projects.

14. At the end of the day, make a to-do list for tomorrow while it's fresh in your head. That way you will hit the ground running in the morning.

This has been an important chapter to help you hone your resilience skills and look after your health and wellbeing. After all, without our health, we are fit for nothing.

There is one final point about wellbeing: humour. We truly need to lighten up and have fun to stay mentally well. I feel so strongly about this that I have dedicated a whole chapter to having fun at work and why it's one of the best ways to communicate in business. But try not to jump directly to Chapter 6 now, because the next step in the *Your Brain is Boss* journey to success is to understand and use emotional intelligence, which is the next chapter. Emotional intelligence is a vital skill that will make your job interviews shine and will certainly help you develop a business of your own. In fact, you can bet your bottom dollar that your competition is honing their emotional intelligence skills right now. Don't be left behind.

Chapter 3
Upgrade your skills
Emotional intelligence, emotional literacy, emotional labour

Chapter 3
Upgrade your skills
Emotional intelligence, emotional literacy, emotional labour

> **Emotional intelligence is *the* single most important skill you need in business today.**

It is argued that emotional intelligence is *the* single most important skill you need to succeed in this fast-paced world. It is hard to find the time to stand back and consider how we interact with people and build strong relationships. But just look around you. Have you noticed how some people with an impressive portfolio of qualifications and experience still struggle to earn a decent living? Have you noticed how the most talented people often have to do various different jobs to make ends meet? And have you ever watched less qualified, less experienced, less talented people earning well, happy and healthy? Annoying, isn't it?

Why? The answer is probably that they have a high level of emotional intelligence (referred to as EQ).

Emotional intelligence isn't a mysterious thing that has only become trendy in recent years. In fact, the first recorded reference to emotional intelligence was by clinical professor of psychology and psychiatry, Michael Beldoch in 1964. The idea was developed further by German psychiatrist Leuner in 1966 and momentum built through further research work by Harvard Professor of Education Howard Gardner on multiple intelligences in 1983. That momentum continues to this day.

Emotional intelligence is a valuable addition to the *Your Brain is Boss* kitbag that you can learn and improve upon. Companies are increasingly looking to fill vacant roles with candidates who are comfortable with emotional intelligence and can show that they know how to use it. In the privacy of this book, you can learn how to use emotion as a method to collect useful data on what is going on around and within you. When you understand this, you can use the information to recognise problems, think clearly to change things and communicate with clarity and ease. These are important steps towards influencing others.

There is, however, a lot more to understanding emotion in business. Emotional literacy and emotional labour are two areas that are rarely talked about, but they are just as useful when hiring people and working with diverse groups of colleagues, clients and customers.

Emotional intelligence, emotional literacy and emotional labour are all similar and yet different at the same time. Each one deserves a dedicated book of its own, but the important thing is for you to read enough in order to implement positive changes straight away. To this end, we will cover each topic in turn and break it down to key components for you to use with ease.

Emotional intelligence

EQ – to understand and control your own emotions; to understand the emotions of others in order to adapt your response and communicate better.

We are living in an age of isolation and virtual relationships. Armies of workers sit in front of a screen all day entering data, emailing, texting or whatever the latest mode of communication is, and often that's just to the person sitting next to them! Of course, this increasing reliance on technologies is essential in the global market, but more than ever before, companies and corporations are realising that not only do we need to be equipped with skills to handle and adapt well to change (adaptability and resilience – perspective, interpersonal skills), but we also need to be masters at collaboration and team building (rapport, empathy, cooperation – communication skills). Add to this the need for us all to be self-sufficient (initiative, motivation, leadership potential) and you have a mix of essential, transferable business skills and leadership qualities that actually make a concrete difference to the success of individuals and the profitability of any business.

But do not fret! There are ways to develop and polish these talents under one umbrella – emotional intelligence. As we learn to handle our own emotional responses and become increasingly more aware of other people's emotional states, using empathy and self-awareness, our level of EQ will get better and our value as an employee or leader will improve enormously.

However, you need to feel motivated to develop and grow. To truly improve your EQ, effort and self-awareness are necessary, but the rewards are worth it, no matter where you are in the hierarchy of the business world, for in order to climb the corporate ladder or build your own business, EQ is the single most important skill to develop.

By being emotionally intelligent you can gather emotional *intelligence*.

A case study of JB

If you are an aspiring business leader or already a manager or leader and want to improve, a fine example of excellent leadership came from a CEO I interviewed a while ago. We will call him JB. Within a year of taking up the post, he had virtually doubled the headcount and business was booming. With that kind of track record, I wanted to know more about him and how he had made such a difference in a short space of time. I also wanted to know what the board thought of the situation, so I started my interview process with them.

I spoke to each C-level executive on the board in turn and was amazed that, without exception, they began by complaining about JB. They told me he was a great guy and business had never been better, but working with him was 'driving them nuts'. How could such a successful CEO upset so many on his main team? I'm sure you are imagining what they said next, but you may be surprised by their answers.

One by one, they complained that JB wasn't interested in spreadsheets and graphs, all he wanted to talk about was how the employees felt and what their thoughts were. In fact, when I interviewed JB he told me he spent most of his day talking to the staff, trying to find out how he could help them, what they needed, what they thought of the products, what they thought of the competition, what the customers were saying out on the street, what personal aspirations they had, were they looking for promotion at some stage, how their families were, where they liked to go on holiday... the list seemed endless.

There is no doubt that JB had a high EQ, and there is no doubt from what I observed and was told that business was booming since he took over.

Basically, JB focused on people and not on technology. As wonderful as technology is, he said, it is just a tool. His focus was on the needs of his staff and customers. JB spent all his time engaging with others and in so doing he could gauge their responses, and use this data in order to influence relevant outcomes that suited everyone. In other words, he gathered emotional *intelligence* through being emotionally intelligent himself and thus created a powerful impact.

It's an interesting way of looking at things, isn't it? Intelligence doesn't just mean our capacity to learn and understand things, it also means to gather and distribute information, and JB was highly adept at both.

Emotional intelligence and emotional *intelligence*

'I only want to make money and save money'. OK, but you will be so much better at that by using emotional intelligence.

'I'm not interested in all that emotion stuff, the only thing I'm interested in is how to make money and save money.' If I had £1 for every time I heard a senior business person say something like this, I would be far richer. The problem stems from the popular view that rational business people are damned if they succumb to displays of emotion. Of course, allowing emotions to get out of control is something to be avoided; all hell can break loose if negative things are said that can never be unsaid. But this is one of the reasons to become better at emotional intelligence, in order to control emotion, both within yourself and others, rather than emotion controlling you.

Emotions are processed in an older part of the brain, mostly in the limbic system. This primitive area facilitates intuitive behaviour, and this was the only way humans used to process information in order to survive and thrive long ago. Emotions were the boss then and often still are today. Evolution has moved our biology along quite a distance and we now have a glorious frontal lobe in the brain that facilitates executive functions such as decision making, judgement, problem solving, attention, planning, reasoning and so on. Many people are under the impression that this delicious mechanism is the new boss, but this isn't necessarily so. This topic will be explored in more detail in Chapter 5 on decision making. For the purposes of this chapter, however, the key to the relationship between emotion and higher executive functions is that we can learn and develop emotional intelligence in order to allow the frontal lobe a bit more control over those knee-jerk emotions that can otherwise (a) get us into trouble and (b) stop us from communicating and becoming a person of influence.

So let's get to grips with EQ and develop this fertile area of business acumen.

Daniel Goleman, author of the bestselling book *Emotional Intelligence* (1995), divided EQ into five key components. Self-awareness, self-regulation, self-motivation (looking inward), empathy and social skills (looking outward).

Self-awareness – recognising and understanding our own emotions

Emotions are a barometer of how you are feeling at any one time. They are fleeting messages, micro alarms that you need to be aware of. When you notice and understand your emotional reactions, you will be proficient at self-awareness. This skill is highly useful for you to recognise whether you are going in the right direction, and it is the first step towards you being in control by stepping back and noticing the emotion. When we assess ourselves accurately, we are automatically more confident.

> **Self-awareness is the first step to improving emotional intelligence.**

Action steps: how to improve self-awareness

1. Ask yourself what you are feeling.
2. Stop and pay attention to what triggered the emotion. Remember, your reaction was your choice.
3. Write down your thoughts.
4. Keep these notes for a short while and look back at them to see if you can spot a pattern. You are now developing self-awareness.
5. Don't keep notes for long: they are a learning tool and not to dwell upon. So destroy them and begin again if you need to.

Self-regulation – regulating and managing our own emotions

What are your core values? To help you know what they are, imagine someone is disrespectful about something that is important to you and it leaves you feeling anxious or even worse. An example might be that you saw someone deliberately kick a puppy. If you felt troubled, angry or anxious, then kindness or fairness is probably one of your core values, what is truly important to you.

Honouring your core values will be second nature, so if someone violates what is deeply important to you, no matter what you are doing at the time, you will know how to respond to larger ethical or moral issues. This in itself is empowering because you will be acting authentically and in your long-term best interests.

Self-regulation means using this flexibility and it also means being accountable and not blaming others. A CEO once told me 'you only have to apologise for the truth once'. This is something for us all to remember. If you face up to mistakes quickly and honestly, it will be as painless as it can be and people will admire and respect you far more.

> **'You only have to apologise for the truth once.'**
> *Peter Manning*

Action steps: how to improve self-regulation

1. Make a list of your core values: what is important to you. This will help you know who you are at a deeper level and will show you what you will not compromise on.

2. Get in the habit of admitting your mistakes. Others will follow your leadership with admiration.

3. Next time you are angry or upset, step outside of yourself as if you are standing next to you. What do you look like?

Is your face crumpled and distorted with temper? It's not a good look, is it? If that doesn't defuse the situation, go to number 4.

4. Rather than shout at someone, take a breath and write down your frustrations. But as before, never keep these notes. Put them in the shredding machine out of harm's way.

5. Seeing yourself angry and reading your tirades helps you evaluate your responses and is an effective way to regulate your behaviour.

6. This isn't just about regulating your negative behaviour, it's also about regulating or improving your positive behaviour by making yourself feel better. How about taking a walk or remembering a time when you felt good?

Self-motivation – being enthusiastic, interested and driven

Self-motivated people consistently drive towards achievement. They are optimistic, positive and committed.

Self-motivated people are driven to achieve well, to improve all the time, to take the initiative and to seize opportunities. They are realistically optimistic. They are resilient and use their time wisely (see Chapter 2). A key to their success is that they welcome feedback and use it to progress.

Are you as self-motivated as you would like to be? Perhaps you once were, but things have waned a little. If so, take a look at these how-to's.

Action steps: how to improve self-motivation

1. Consider why you originally took the job you are in now. Remember how you felt and why you felt that way on your first day. Has anything changed for the better or for the worse? Think carefully.

2. If you need a 'reboot', how about re-evaluating your goals. Are they achievable? Do they excite you? If not, change them.

3. If you are spending too much time with negative people, seek out people who have a zest for life. Enthusiasm is contagious.

4. Find a like-minded friend who you can confide in. Challenge each other to find something positive out of every setback you each encounter, no matter how big or small. Make sure you hold each other accountable on this one.

5. If you can't think of a friend to do this with, then monitor your own behaviour. Notice if you are doom and gloom or if you see an opportunity in setbacks. Practise finding the silver lining.

Empathy – sensing the emotions that drive people's behaviour

Empathy enables greater understanding and allows us to communicate better.

Empathy is the ability to put yourself in the other person's shoes, to feel how they are feeling on some level (but remember you will not know *exactly* how they feel; that is neither possible nor necessary – see introduction on perception). Empathy is not to be confused with sympathy, which is feeling compassion for someone and feeling sorry that they are having a difficult time. Empathy is about sensing how someone may be feeling and is a skill that can be learnt. When we have empathy, we have a deeper understanding of others and this enables us to communicate better and be of greater service.

Empathy is written about in more detail in Chapter 2, but in case you skipped that part, let's touch upon it briefly here.

A colleague or boss who shows empathy will develop a culture of trust, loyalty and respect, which comes from caring for others. For instance, perhaps you know someone at work who has a child with special needs and has various hospital appointments to go to. It's hard for them to juggle work, their emotional roller-coaster and taking extra time off. They are probably riddled with guilt and worried for their job. But if you could, for instance, alleviate some of the pressure by offering to help them catch up with a backlog of work, then not only would you be showing a huge amount of empathy, but business will run more smoothly and your colleague will value your friendship even more.

Empathy is not culturally specific, it embraces diversity and political awareness. Having empathy for our fellow human beings leads to understanding and excellent communication. I can't think of a better way to avoid conflict at work.

Action steps: how to build more empathy

1. Practise listening to people and try to understand and remember what they have said.

2. Look at body language. Non-verbal communication is important. For instance, does someone look hunched up and smaller than normal? If so, ask if they are OK.

3. Try to see things from their point of view. There is never only one way to look at a situation.

4. Practise noticing other people. Watch for signs of someone overworking and getting flustered. Offer to help.

5. Say thank you. If someone has done something for you, show your appreciation.

Social skills – interpersonal skills that progress positive communication with others

Social skills are not mystical, they are necessary and can be improved upon.

There are some people in this world who are exceptionally good at social skills. They can get the best out of people; they are not afraid of bad news, they listen with an open mind, collaborate and communicate and come up with a solution; they know how to build a cooperative team; they manage change and conflict as part of their daily tasks; they know when to leave things alone if they are working, preferring the adage 'if it ain't broke don't fix it'. As such, they are great influencers.

Again, according to Goleman, all of these skills can be learnt. If you want to improve your social skills try a few of these pointers.

Action steps: how to improve social skills

1. If there is one thing everyone wants to feel, it is *significant*. Show people how important you think their work is.
2. Also show fairness, but never favouritism.
3. Learn how to praise others appropriately in a way that suits each person. For instance, some people like public praise while others would recoil at the idea and prefer a quiet 'well done'.
4. Express yourself clearly. Ask yourself what your objectives are for this conversation.
5. Adjust your conversation depending on who you are speaking to.
6. Try to anticipate people's reactions and be as prepared as you can be, while choosing your words carefully.
7. If your conversation is sensitive, go to a quiet office so that you are not disturbed.
8. Don't interrupt, and let people know you are listening by nodding appropriately.
9. If there is a problem, deal with it immediately, don't let it fester.
10. Acknowledge a problem, and talk about it so that everyone involved realises it too.

11. If there is a team issue, talk about the impact of the issue on the team and make sure all discussions are for the good of the team.

12. Practise, practise, practise being clear and fair.

13. Remember, the best lessons are caught not taught, so be the person you want others to be.

Emotional *intelligence*

> ### Never underestimate emotional data and the impact it can have on business.

This is quite a comprehensive list of ideas to enable you to improve your emotional intelligence. But what about emotional *intelligence*? Consider JB in our case study. His emotional intelligence traits were excellent while at the same time he was collecting valuable data about the emotional state of his employees, what people and customers thought about their products, what the competition was doing, what people were gossiping about.

You may think gossip has nothing to do with business. But you only have to look at the effect that Twitter can have on a company's reputation to know that throwaway remarks can damage reputations enormously. So JB was rather clever in collecting so much data that could have an effect on the business. Intelligence, even at an emotional level, is worth collecting.

Action steps: how to gather emotional *intelligence*

1. As part of your efforts in improving your emotional intelligence, engage people in conversations that seemingly have little to do with work. Their insights, although not directly about business, may offer vital clues as to what the market is doing or the level of job satisfaction amongst the staff.

2. The observations you can make through interpersonal contact like this can have strong value, but that doesn't mean you are being sneaky, it means you are being genuinely interested and value their opinion, so be upfront and transparent. However, please diplomatically check any data with other sources to make sure the person wasn't just having a bad day.

3. Perhaps you could ask a question such as 'what is the greatest lesson you have learnt while working here?' The answers may offer insight into underlying issues you are not aware of.

4. Another useful thing to ask is if they know anyone who they think you should know. Perhaps they could introduce you. This is a great way to build a meaningful network.

Emotional intelligence is a massive topic and emotional *intelligence* is an additional way of developing in this area. If you would like to know more about EQ, a suggested reading list is included at the end of the book. I hope you have found these ideas useful so far, but we haven't finished yet. Let's take a brief look at emotional literacy and see if you can use this to develop and grow.

Emotional literacy

> **Emotional literacy focuses on cooperation and the common good.**

It's worth being aware of emotional literacy if you want to continue mastering personal growth. Emotional literacy appears very similar to EQ, but there are differences.

EQ focuses on the individual, whereas emotional literacy focuses on other people as well. Psychotherapist Claude Steiner refers to it as 'emotional intelligence with a heart'. The concept helps people develop cooperation and consider the common good. For instance, the common good of a group of people from different cultures.

Emotional literacy is a humanistic approach that envelopes equality and social justice, always important topics. According to author Brian Matthews, a person who is proficient at emotional literacy interacts well with groups of people from different backgrounds, perhaps of a different sexual orientation, different ethnic background, the opposite gender, or different social class.

If you want to improve your capability in this area, may I first suggest you read an emotional literacy book by Claude Steiner such as *Emotional Literacy: Intelligence with a heart* (2003), as well as an educational perspective by Brian Matthews called *Engaging Education: Developing emotional literacy, equity and co-education* (2006).

And second, go back to the 'how-to' sections above and continue to work on them with diverse groups of people and embrace working groups as a whole. For instance, if there is a team issue, talk about its impact on the team and make sure all discussions are for the good of the team.

Emotional labour

> **If the emotions you want your people to display with customers are not part of their natural profile, it could be a disaster.**

Emotional labour is an extremely important topic that is often overlooked. Emotional labour refers to the feelings and expressions of emotion that are needed for someone to do their job properly.

For instance, when I owned and ran a health club, one of my receptionists simply could not bring herself to smile. No matter what I did to encourage her, her negative expression actually put off potential new members from joining. This was a big problem. It was a requirement of the job for the receptionists to smile when people walked through the door, but she couldn't do it. Sometimes she did try, but the effect was inauthentic and she experienced dissonance between the emotions she was feeling and the emotions she was required to display. This was dysfunctional for her and for the business because she couldn't manage her emotional expression when interacting with the customers.

Here's another situation to consider. Imagine you work at Disney World in Florida. Here, one of the primary objectives of all the staff is to make the visitors feel playful and happy. Inducing those feelings in others if you don't feel them yourself is almost impossible and likely to be emotionally draining for you. Of course, we all have bad days, but if the situation persisted you might conclude you were not suited to the job.

If, however, you are a naturally quiet person with a great deal of empathy, then perhaps you are best suited to work in a hospital or as a social worker. Or maybe you love clothes and styling so would be efficient and effective in a fashion store.

Can you see where this is going?

Emotional labour refers to managing and regulating your emotions in accordance with the objectives of the job and the company. If these are misaligned, both the company and the employee are likely to suffer. This is especially important if the work is in the service industry. It is therefore an extremely good idea if you follow these suggestions.

1. Find work that suits your emotional disposition.
2. When recruiting staff who are customer facing, use interview techniques that allow you to measure the emotional suitability of the candidate (having first established what your organisation's needs are).

3. If you are building a business, you will save yourself a lot of time and money if you address this issue up front. Emotional dissonance can be costly.

An excellent book on the subject is by Alicia Grandey and colleagues – *Emotional Labor in the 21st Century: Diverse perspectives on emotional regulation at work* (2013). This book will help you especially if you are an entrepreneur and want to hit the ground running.

In summary, emotional intelligence is a vital skill. In the fast-moving world of today, those who are EQ proficient will succeed beyond their colleagues who are not so adept. EQ helps you control your responses and interactions with people, thus enabling far better communication. *Your Brain Is* becoming a far better *Boss*.

There are, of course, other transferable skills that you can master that will certainly help you become more sought after and influential. In the next chapter we will take a look at improving problem-solving skills and our ability to be more creative. Can you imagine mastering these as well? There will be no stopping you!

Chapter 4
Becoming exceedingly valuable
Problem solving and creative thinking

Chapter 4
Becoming exceedingly valuable
Problem solving and creative thinking

Intuition is subliminal processing based on implicit knowledge (unconscious).

A senior firefighter was watching his men enter an industrial building. There was a fire inside, but one of his men radioed out to say that it was contained and they had it under control.

All of a sudden, the senior firefighter shouted down the radio to his men, 'Get out! Get out now!'

They were surprised. 'It's OK. We've got it covered.'

'That's an order – get out now, fast!'

As the last man ran out of the door, the building exploded.

The senior firefighter had saved the lives of everyone through what seemed like his intuition.

But was it?

After much investigation, it was concluded that he unconsciously recognised the way the smoke was behaving as he had experienced the same circumstances years before when he was a junior firefighter. A building had exploded, and just before the explosion, the smoke had behaved in a specific way. He hadn't registered it as such at the time, but when trying to recall what had alerted him to the dangers of the most recent incident, he realised that somewhere deep in his unconscious, he had recognised that the smoke was behaving in exactly the same way as it had all those years ago, although he didn't realise it at the time. He saved his men by remembering – below conscious awareness – the same subtle danger signs, a long-forgotten memory deep in his unconscious mind.

This story was reported on a TV documentary some time ago.

There are always problems to solve: customer problems, client problems, staff problems, technical problems, problems at home. Problems are everywhere. Some of them we don't really notice as problems because they occur frequently so we are used to fixing them and just getting on with it.

If, however, we focus too much on problems that are harder to fix, we can become bogged down and find it difficult to think clearly. In this situation, we have a tendency to focus on what has already happened and may even look to blame others or make excuses about why we haven't come up with any answers. This is highly stressful and useless in the workplace. On the other hand, if we can focus on the future and come up with solutions, this is less stressful and we become exceedingly valuable. This means we are forward focusing, looking for ways out, enjoying the process and happy to take responsibility for the results.

That's what this chapter is about: offering some examples and advice on problem solving and creative thinking, to help you hone your own problem-solving skills in order to become even more valuable and avoid burning out. Imagine what it will be like to have a template to work with so that you handle problems well and come up with creative ideas. And not only that, imagine what it will be like to mentor your team to do the same.

Instinct is an innate behaviour, it is automatic and needs no training. It is a genetically hardwired behaviour like a bird building a nest.

Creative thinking – where would we be without it?

What comes into your mind when you think of creativity? An artist painting beautiful works of art? A designer with imagination and skills for contemporary architecture? An original thinker of the type lauded as a genius? Of course, creativity is all of these, but creative people also think of valuable and practical ways of doing things. They solve problems on a regular basis by employing creative thought. That is the kind of creativity we are going to discuss now, another skill you can develop to be more influential at work so that you become trusted and well respected. An asset to any company.

Graham Wallas, social psychologist and co-founder of the London School of Economics, developed a theory of a creative process that I think you may find useful. With observations some years earlier from Poincaré, a French mathematician (1913), Wallas came up with a logical and practical template to harness the seemingly illogical unconscious thinking that can nevertheless be so illuminating and turn into the perfect solution to problems (1926).

There are four steps to this model:

1. Preparation – recognise the problem and find out as much about it as you can. Consciously try to come up with an answer.
2. Incubation – do something unrelated to the problem. Think of something else and allow your mind to unconsciously work on the problem.
3. Illumination – it is during the incubation period that an unrelated event could give an answer, a sort of realisation, an illumination.
4. Verification – at this point you check the solution you have come up with to see if it will work.

The 'incubation' period is the interesting part, and this has stimulated much debate over the years. It could be that the information you consider in the preparation phase has itself already undergone some unconscious processing. Some believe that unconscious thinking is faster than conscious thought, so is therefore more efficient in the incubation phase. More recently, psychologists such as Simonton have suggested that unconscious processing is more effective than conscious processing because it does not have the constraints associated with normal concepts, so frees the mind to come up with novel answers (Simonton, 1999).

As is often the case in psychology, researchers such as Weisberg (2006) disagree, and the incubation period model is disputed. Many believe that problem solving isn't in the least bit mysterious and is a combination of relevant knowledge, factual information and problem-solving strategies. In this context, these strategies can include analogical problem solving whereby we use our experiences of similar situations and apply this previously acquired knowledge to find solutions. This makes sense, but no two situations will ever be identical, so it's wise to stay open-minded and be flexible.

A recent study by Saggar and colleagues (2015) found a link between creative problem solving and activity in the cerebellum part of the brain, which is normally associated with regulating motor movements such as balance, coordination and speech. The researchers also referred to the cerebellum as the 'practice-makes-perfect' centre. They found that when people engaged the executive-control centre, engaging higher-order functions such as planning and organising, it actually impaired creative problem solving. In this instance, thinking logically didn't help with the task.

For complex problems that appear to have multiple answers: divergent and convergent thinking

American psychologist Joy Paul Guilford suggested that divergent thinking means focusing on a problem in a creative way (1950). Brainstorming is an example of divergent thinking, as is free writing. Divergent thinking allows abstract thought, thinking outside the box and coming up with new ideas. This is an ideal way to solve problems that are complex and have multiple ways of looking at things. For instance, sometimes unexpected combinations of ideas can be enlightening. When I was considering the title of this book, I made several Mind Maps. Here is one of them. As you see, I wrote down unexpected combinations of words, starting with 'brain'.

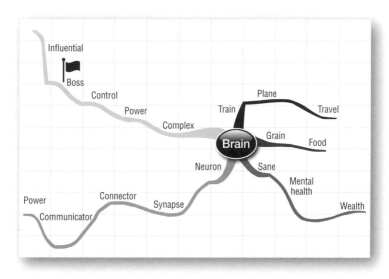

Mind Map made in coming up with the title of this book

I then took all the information and ideas and organised them in order to find one single solution. In so doing, this exercise then shifted to become one of convergent thinking.

Convergent thinking is based on knowledge, facts, no ambiguity and finding the best single answer. It's when we work out a solution in a deliberate, logical fashion.

An efficient and productive way of using divergent thinking for open-ended, complex problems and allowing for creativity is to combine it with convergent thinking, in order to find a single answer and convert that into a practical application.

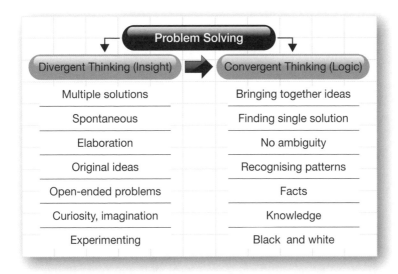

Problem Solving		
Divergent Thinking (Insight)		**Convergent Thinking (Logic)**
Multiple solutions		Bringing together ideas
Spontaneous		Finding single solution
Elaboration		No ambiguity
Original ideas		Recognising patterns
Open-ended problems		Facts
Curiosity, imagination		Knowledge
Experimenting		Black and white

Divergent and convergent thinking in problem solving

In my example of naming this book, I took the data from my various scribblings and thought about the one thing I wanted to help the readers with. I wanted you to have a better level of mental health (Chapter 2); I wanted you to attain greater wealth to get on those aeroplanes and travel far and wide; I wanted you to become even better at communication; I wanted you to feel powerful at work. The one word that did all of this and more was for you to become the boss of you. And so my problem of finding a title for this book was solved by using divergent and convergent thinking. This gave me a deeper understanding of the problem, and from my scribblings I could clearly derive the answer I wanted – *Your Brain is Boss* was born.

Insight – 'Aha!' can also come from trial and error

You could argue that by bringing together divergent and convergent thinking, I gained insight into the problem I was trying to solve. Insight is a sudden clarity, a pattern recognition connecting the answer with the problem. It's like an 'Aha!' moment, when you suddenly see the whole answer.

> **Insight is a deep understanding followed by suddenly seeing a pattern and the realisation of what the answer is. An 'Aha!' moment.**

I saw an example of insight used effectively to establish and resolve a business problem when undertaking a project with a mid-sized client company. The client was involved in the acquisition of a smaller company operating in the same business, generally dealing with smaller customers. A key operational problem to be tackled was how to integrate the two company systems.

The first thing the acquiring management team naturally did was to take in all the known information and make a mental picture of the problem. They also imagined taking on a disgruntled workforce, not wanting to integrate, resistant to learning new systems imposed on them and worrying that there might be some redundancies. Unless the staff could be made to feel at ease, they would not learn the new systems easily and there could be a large number of angry customers to contend with.

So the acquiring management team had formed their own internal representation of the problem based on the information they had. But there was a lot of detail still missing, like personalities and capabilities and so on. Still, they worked on the task to try to come up with a solution, but after much effort spent in thinking and discussing this, they were bogged down and had not come up with satisfactory answers.

Failing at the task was not an option, as this would have diminished or negated the value of the acquisition. Therefore, they finally achieved a solution to their problem by going back to basics, gathering more information (elaborating) so that a new internal representation of the problem could be formed (re-encoding).

They decided to study closely the systems being used in the smaller company and run a detailed comparison with those in use in their own company. With the similarities and the differences clearly defined and understood, a short training manual was drawn up that 'spoke their language'.

According to psychology professor Ohlsson, the solution was easy once they had relaxed their self-imposed constraints of worrying about the personalities of people they had not yet met and had rethought what the problem actually was in terms of integrating the two systems (1992).

If we get stuck when trying to solve a problem, it is sometimes useful to think about the problem in a totally different way in order to gain insight and achieve that 'Aha!' moment.

Self-imposed constraints sometimes sabotage progress. Don't be afraid to go back to the beginning with fresh information.

How to stimulate divergent thinking

Do you ever enjoy wallowing in bed when you first wake up in the morning? You know, when you are not quite awake but no longer fully asleep. It's a delicious moment to allow your mind to wander. At this time, your brain is in alpha frequency. We can achieve the same frequency when we are staring out of the window, or watching the rain fall. It is during times like these when a solution to a problem seems to come from nowhere. Therefore, one of the best ways to stimulate divergent thinking is to put the brain in alpha frequency, so much so that it's worth keeping a notepad handy to capture those thoughts before they fade away.

As I had touched on earlier, the billions of neurons in our brain communicate with one another in one of two ways. Either by chemicals or by electricity passing a signal from one neuron to another via a dynamic connection called a synapse.

To recap from Chapter 2 and for ease of reference: electrical signals between neurons work in harmony and create a neural network. This activity is called a brainwave. Brainwaves have different frequencies.

- Gamma waves (25–100 Hz, typically 40 Hz): the fastest pattern of neural oscillations associated with conscious perception.
- Beta waves (12–25 Hz): alert and focused, our normal awake state. Studies show that if we get stuck in this frequency we can become depressed or anxious.
- Alpha waves (8–12 Hz): daydreaming, meditating. Associated with creative thought.
- Theta waves (3–8 Hz): REM sleep and a deep meditation that practised meditators can achieve.
- Delta waves (0.5–3 Hz): the slowest frequency achieved when we are in deep dreamless sleep.

If we wish to stimulate creative thought and innovation in our teams, it is useful to encourage allowing the mind to wander. This can slow the brain down and relax the stress of relentlessly focusing on a particular problem.

Not to relax in some way is actually counterproductive to problem solving. When we are anxious or feeling stressed, the brain is wired to think it's under threat. When this happens, our focus is closed down to facilitate maximum concentration on dealing with this perceived threat. This is a survival instinct: through the ages of Homo sapiens it has been essential to pay full attention to what can harm us so that we can keep ourselves safe. However, if the brain's perceived threat is not a life-or-death situation but we are actually involved with a problem at work, the last thing you want to do is constrain your thinking in a state of anxiety. When we are relaxed, when we are having fun, when we find things funny, we open up our thinking and are in a much better state to find creative solutions (see more about the efficacy of fun at work in Chapter 6).

Creative thinking works best when we are relaxed, having fun and able to laugh.

While on the subject of putting yourself in the optimum state for problem solving, never underestimate the importance of sleep. I'm sure you have experienced the effect that a restless night has on your productivity the next day. When we don't sleep well we function in a state of 'brain fog' and are sometimes barely able to complete the day's tasks. And as for innovation and creativity – you can forget it. It's just not going to happen.

A good night's sleep will help you come up with creative and innovative ideas. Relax.

The benefits of sufficient sleep add more evidence in support of approaching problems in a relaxed, positive frame of mind because this will result in us naturally sleeping better too. Truly a virtuous circle.

Action steps: how to increase your chances of insight (individually)

1. Relax, go for a walk, enjoy what's around you.
2. Watch a funny film or video clip.
3. Review the problem, but don't tackle it until you feel in a good mood.
4. If it's too hard, stop. Get out of the office and do something that doesn't take any concentration. Feed the birds, go for a bike ride.
5. When the answer appears, write it down.

6. Tell those who are involved. They will probably feel relieved, but be careful not to brag.
7. Congratulate yourself for solving the problem. The 'feel-good' neurochemicals stimulated in the brain will encourage you to do it again.

How to encourage insight in others (teams)

When we come together as a team we put pressure on the group to perform. This is rarely satisfactory as what invariably happens is that there are those who regularly participate, those who feel they are not worthy to participate and are often ignored, and those who are bored and have little to offer.

In actual fact, it is better to gather collective thinking once everyone has had time to think by themselves. Otherwise there is the danger of typical group dynamics resulting in the loss of potential pearls of wisdom from team members who may not fully engage or participate.

Perhaps next time you have a situation where you want your team to come up with solutions, it may be better to talk about the problem as a group. Everyone then separates and follows the ideas above for individuals. Then the team comes together again to collect divergent ideas as well as the more logical data from the convergent thinkers. The follow-up group session can be turned into a convergent think tank to generate the best answers.

Get everyone to think about a problem individually. Then come together to brainstorm it.

How to help others who have a problem to solve

Sometimes a colleague or member of staff has a problem to solve. It may not be part of your job, but you feel compelled to help. A simple conversation may be all it takes to help them, but this may be taken the wrong way. You might inadvertently make them feel inadequate because they are struggling. This is especially so if they are feeling anxious. So tread carefully.

You could, for instance, ask 'Do you want to talk this through?' This will give them the option of saying 'No thank you' and maintaining their dignity or saying 'Yes, I would appreciate the opportunity to use you as a sounding board.' If the conversation carries on, you may know of some information that would be useful or think of someone you know who could help. Again, ask permission, so that you don't take control. For instance, 'I may have a piece of information that you might find useful' or 'I may know someone who can help. Would you like to know more?'

Always be mindful of helping people feel *significant* too. They will remember and appreciate you for it.

> **When helping someone solve a problem, ask if they want to talk it through. Be mindful that they want to feel *significant* too.**

Whether you prefer a logical way of solving problems or a more insightful way of creating solutions, it is likely that you will not be purely in one camp or the other. For you to be most valuable, perhaps the most effective strategy is to be open-minded and try all of these ideas for various problems as they arise. You will then probably find that your problem-solving kitbag is versatile and efficient and you feel a lot better by having greater control of how you contribute at work.

Of course, problem solving is only part of the story. Understanding how to make better decisions will round off this topic well. This is what we are going to cover next.

Action steps: how to improve your problem-solving skills

1. Use Wallas's four-step model to see if it works for you.

2. Think of a similar experience you have had and see if it works this time, but stay open-minded. The situation will not be identical.

3. Brainstorm your own ideas by making a Mind Map or list of anything that comes into your mind in relation to the problem.

4. Transfer your thinking into convergent thinking, first by a process of elimination and then with a new short list to hone the solution.

5. Self-imposed constraints can stop you coming up with solutions. If you are stuck, go back to unearth new information or be prepared to look at it differently.

6. When your brain is in alpha frequency, keep a notepad nearby to capture all those wonderful ideas.

7. Relaxation, laughter and fun are not self-indulgent, they are tools that will make you much better at problem solving.

8. A good night's sleep is a priority. Brain fog is not useful. Get to bed.

9. For team insight, inform everyone of the problem and let them go away to think about it. Remember that they too need to be in a positive frame of mind to figure out solutions. Then come together and brainstorm everyone's ideas.

10. If someone needs help solving a problem, ask their permission to lend a hand. Help them feel *significant* too.

Chapter 5
**Powering up
Reasoning and
superb decision making**

Chapter 5
Powering up
Reasoning and superb decision making

Have you noticed how many poor decisions are being made every day? A combination of procrastination, uncertainty, panic decisions, not having enough information and closed minds choosing not to see better alternatives. Not to mention possible anxiety and conflict. Sometimes it's hard work making decisions and extremely costly when we make the wrong ones.

In our belief that we can make rational decisions we try to put steps in place that are logical and fit for every eventuality. But this is futile. Partly because we are not as rational as we like to think we are and partly because every situation is different. Your brain can play tricks and we need to be aware and learn in order to better control this amazing biological creation, the brain.

A case in point is Sam. Having worked all weekend, Sam was pleased with himself. He worked on data, graphs and a logical argument to close a deal he had been working on for some time. At 9 am on Monday morning, Sam sent the proposal across to the customer. They had a good relationship, so Sam waited comfortably in the certainty that this piece of work matched their needs exactly.

A day went by and Sam started to get worried, knowing that the customer had to make a decision quickly. He called the customer. He got straight through. He didn't get the deal. Totally shocked, Sam asked why.

'I liked the proposal, Sam, but you just didn't get where we are coming from. You didn't seem to understand us. It's hard to put my finger on, but we've decided to go with someone else.'

Sam didn't understand why they seemed to have made such an irrational decision. Poor Sam.

More than ever before, decision making is becoming increasingly important in the success or failure of a business. The breakneck speed with which companies grow, are acquired, and need to change in brutally unforgiving markets is highly unlikely to slow down.

Influential people are not only excellent at making decisions, they are also excellent at making decisions that others understand and support. But did you know that studies show we can't actually make a rational decision without an emotional response?

Sam relied on technical and accurate persuasions. But by appealing only to cognition, Sam didn't engage emotionally. Emotion is the persuader, the influencer. This chapter will look at the role emotion plays in decision making and discuss other apparent quirks in our behaviour that seem to be almost mysterious when it comes to how people make decisions. From heuristics, biases, gut feelings, attention, irrationality and various reasoning models, you will learn the different ways people make decisions, how best to use your own strengths when it comes to decisions and how you can influence others to make decisions that benefit everyone. We will also cover when it's best not to make a decision at all.

Let's begin with emotion and decision making.

Emotion and decision making

An interesting study by the eminent neuroscientist Professor Antonio Damasio investigated the effect of emotion on decision making (2001). This research came from his work over many years with patients who had sustained head injuries.

Some of his patients had damage to the prefrontal cortex (PFC) in their brains, the area which is principally involved in higher executive functions such as planning, decision making, judgements and more. Damage to these higher-order functions meant that his patients had lost the connection that translates physical feelings to emotional response – things like sweating, rapid heartbeat and butterflies in the stomach. So when some of Damasio's patients felt these sensations, they didn't understand what they meant because there was no emotional link.

There is an important distinction between emotion and feelings. According to Damasio, emotion is a chemical and neurological response when presented with appropriate stimuli, whereas feelings are private perceptions of the physiological reactions of emotions.

People often think that emotion has nothing to do with cognition, but the brain regions identified with emotional processing, such as the amygdala, show extensive connections with areas identified with cognition such as the PFC.

In Damasio's view, the experience of emotion begins with conscious considerations that a person holds about someone or something. A cognitive evaluation takes place. This is then signalled to emotion areas in the brain, beginning the coordination of appropriate psychophysiological reactions.

Emotional processing in patients with damage to the PFC means that they cannot generate emotions or 'feelings' relative to images of a situation or stimuli. In the context of these observations, Damasio proffered the *somatic marker hypothesis* (1996). Whether consciously or unconsciously, somatic markers are thought to be stored in the PFC and act as links between cognitive evaluation based on past experiences and a 'feeling' based on emotional signals from the visceral regions (e.g. amygdala and bodily states) which leads to appropriate decision making. From this, Damasio said that 'emotion is an essential element of rational thought', because his patients couldn't make rational decisions without an emotional response. In fact, some of them made some terrible investments and ended up bankrupt, others became dishonest, but most spent endless hours ruminating over irrelevant detail without making a rational decision at all. As a result, he said that 'rationality requires feeling and feeling requires rationality'.

This is a clear message indeed. If we want to understand how we make decisions, we need to realise that rational thinking is modified by emotion. But just to be sure of his findings, Damasio then took his observations into the lab and ran an experiment called 'the Gambling Task'.

The Gambling Task

He gave each healthy participant four decks of cards, two black and two red, plus $2,000 to play with.

Each card in all four decks simply had a sentence printed on one side that told them how much they had won or lost just by the turn of a card.

The participants were instructed to turn over cards in any order they wanted and try to make as much money as possible. This was their only instruction.

Of course, the decks were rigged for experimental purposes but the participants didn't know that. Two decks of cards were high risk (e.g. offering big payouts, but large punishments, such as 'you have won $1,000' or 'you have just lost $1,250'). And two decks were rather conservative, offering smaller payouts with very little forfeit. If they only used the conservative decks they would have made a profit, but this was something they had to work out as they went along. The players didn't know any of this.

After turning over 50 cards, they began unconsciously to use only the profitable decks.

But it took them turning over 80 cards to work out why they favoured those decks.

Meanwhile, during the experiment the participants were wired up to a skin conductance response (SCR) machine where electrodes measured sweat on the palms of their hands to detect nervousness.

> After only turning over 10 cards, the SCR detected nervous-
> ness in the hand when reaching for high-risk cards. So the
> hand knew!

Unconscious feelings govern the conscious mind.

So when people say that emotion doesn't play a part in their decision making, they are not aware that their decisions were already manipulated by emotion below conscious awareness. This shows that there is no getting away from it – *emotion* strongly influences the behaviour of customers, employees, management and peers.

To reiterate from earlier in the book, if you want to influence customers to buy your products, or to influence anybody in any context, remember that emotion drives their decisions. And not only that, some decision making may have happened below awareness. This means that you must make sure – from the very first email, phone call or meeting you have with people – that you always treat them well from the word go.

Emotion influences decisions.

Emotion in advertising

Of course, advertising people have known this for years. They use emotion all the time in advertising campaigns, even below conscious awareness.

I was speaking recently to Tom Goddard, the chairman of Ocean Outdoor, a digital outdoor advertising company, who decided to find out if their methods of working had any scientific foundation. They commissioned an interesting neuroscience project to see if they could measure subliminal emotional processing in their advertising.

Their interpretation of the results was that people were more likely to buy products if they had unconsciously processed the stimuli before and if the second viewing was large, say on a moving screen with emotional content. In other words, when people were exposed to an emotional image without realising it, and then saw it again moving on a large billboard, they were more likely to make a buying decision. They concluded that attention + emotion + memory = influenced buying behaviour.

This was a provocative exercise with views that can be extended to other areas of business such as sales and marketing in order to optimise the return on effort.

Attention + emotion + memory = influenced to buy.

Reasoning

In cognitive psychology, there are four main ways we reason about something:

1. Inductive reasoning: we reach a conclusion generalising or extrapolating from available information (bottom-up logic).
2. Deductive reasoning: think of Sherlock Holmes, he would narrow the evidence under consideration until only the conclusion was left (top-down logic).
3. Analogical thinking: transferring knowledge gained in one situation to a different situation. For instance, 'the last time I went to the doctor's surgery I had to wait an hour. So I had better not make any meetings for the rest of the morning'.
4. Decision making: where we weigh up the information, considering possible outcomes, the risks and the benefits.

It's interesting to note that where you direct your attention will determine whether you make a good decision or not, so it's useful to understand what you tend to focus on when looking at a problem. If your strengths are to weigh things up, but you use deductive reasoning, you may find that you are less efficient. Think about your initial response to solving a problem. The chances are that this is a natural strength for you and is the most valuable way you can contribute to making a decision either for yourself or for your team.

> **Work out your strengths when it comes to reasoning and play to those.**

Decision making

In everyday life we rarely have all the information we need to make a decision. But, even if we could access all the information, would we actually use it all? Say, for instance, you want to hire some external training for your team. You contact several suppliers and they send in proposals. Do you actually compare each proposal thoroughly, taking into account that the various styles of presentation make it hard to compare them accurately, especially as some quotes are opaque while others are more itemised? It's more likely you would get a 'gut feel' for one of the proposals, work out if they can meet your requirements and, if good enough, book them. Satisfaction acquired.

You may feel disappointed reading this, but it's normal. According to pioneer in decision making, Herbert A. Simon, our cognitive system is limited because we can neither process a huge amount of information nor do we have the time to delve deep into our memories to do a thorough evaluation of past relevant knowledge and experience (1957). Instead we take mental shortcuts, known as heuristics. It wasn't until the 1970s that Daniel Kahneman and Amos Tversky built upon Simon's research by conducting experiments in the field with real people in real situations and they discovered that heuristics are not perfect. They said that mental shortcuts focused on only some information while ignoring others, leading to cognitive biases. However, many psychologists, such as Gigerenzer and colleagues (1999), believe that heuristics and biases are a rational means of quickly coming to a decision, even in the absence of all the information.

Pocket history aside, heuristics and biases are something we all use, and being aware of them gives us the power to think more thoroughly about the evidence we are trying to evaluate in order to make a good decision.

Heuristics, biases and how to use them effectively

Quick decisions often come from heuristics, those mental shortcuts that lead to biases. We all have biases when it comes to decision making, and to make things difficult, these biases bubble away below conscious awareness. We are unaware when they sway us in a particular direction, but if we know about them we can make allowances and perhaps come to a better decision than we would otherwise.

The well-known confirmation bias is where we look for information that confirms our thinking. This is hugely apparent when we believe in something and we look for confirmation yet ignore times when our beliefs have not been confirmed. Think about a time at work when you gave a dreadful presentation. You knew it wasn't going well, but you had to keep going. Did you notice the person who was hanging on your every word or did you notice the person on their mobile phone? It is highly likely that because you thought your presentation was going badly you looked for evidence to confirm that belief. Even if 50 per cent of the room were listening intently and 50 per cent were distracted, it would be the latter that you would notice, thus confirming your beliefs.

A heuristic we are all aware of is availability. Using information where we don't consider our personal experiences but instead consider incidents that are embedded in our memory with the efficient help of emotion is called an availability heuristic. It's the shortcut we go to when we read about a crime in graphic detail or a plane crash. Do we now consider the area where the crime took place a serious no-go zone even though we have no personal experience of a problem? Or do we worry about getting on an aeroplane, but it doesn't cross our mind how many accident black spots there are on our drive to work?

Sometimes the infrequency of these dreadful situations bears no relation to a rational evaluation of risk, and in these instances, we become heavily biased about our decisions to enter certain areas or indeed go on an aeroplane.

I had a great-uncle who was convinced that eating meat three times a day and drinking whisky was the secret to a long life. He lived until well into his 80s. On occasion we read stories in the newspapers of elderly people who smoke and drink alcohol daily and, with a glint in their eye, have another glass while blowing out 100 candles from their latest birthday cake. We fall foul of these representational heuristics in thinking that reading a couple of examples provides a recipe for a long life. In order to realistically work out if alcohol, smoking or eating lots of meat will lead to a long life, we would need to look at far more examples than this small representation of the elderly population. Can you see how representative heuristics such as these lead to poor evaluation?

An argument for heuristics is recognition. Imagine you are standing in a shop wanting to buy printing ink. There are two types that you've used before and both are expensive. You will probably think back to the times you have used the two different inks. You may even remember roughly when you put each one in your printer and when you had to replace it. You may even recall that on one particular occasion you did more printing than usual. This quick recognition shortcut would be good enough for you to make a decision about which printing ink would be better value. You would be relying upon remembering your previous experiences and recognising the products, and your decision would have been rational, even though it could be argued it may not be accurate. But it's good enough.

This process may not be perfect, but these cognitive shortcuts allow us to decide things quickly and, in truth, we are not able to calculate everything accurately. So what makes a good decision is one that appears to provide a desired outcome and to do the job, and one that those involved are comfortable with and are willing to implement and/or be accountable for.

Do you cut and run?

Equally, think of a time when you have invested heavily on winning a business project. Many hours, a collection of experts, numerous meetings, proposals, costings, technical input – you have given this a huge amount of effort. But the customer is getting more and more distant and you are continuing to chase and crawl to make it happen, to the point where other projects are suffering. Do you cut your losses and move on? Sometimes that is the sensible thing to do, but more often than not, people think of all of that attachment and don't want to lose it. They are driven to keep going because of loss aversion, avoiding loss rather than considering the gains of letting the project go. This kind of thinking can hinder progress and may be worth being aware of if you are in this situation.

Don't make a decision when you're hungry, tired or too busy!

Like most children, when I was small, I was eager to talk to my father when he got home from work, especially if I wanted something! But I can hear my mother's words to this day: 'Don't ask your father anything until he's eaten.' A wise woman. Even now, I choose not to speak to hungry people if I can avoid doing so.

Little did I know that my mother's warning would be supported by scientific evidence. According to Anderberg and colleagues, the hormone ghrelin, released in the stomach when we are hungry, has an adverse effect on decision making by increasing impulsive behaviour (2015). Therefore, if you have arranged a meeting where decisions need to be made and it's just before lunch, I strongly suggest taking healthy snacks or changing the time of day. Equally, consider this for yourself and try not to put yourself in a decision-making situation unless sated.

And how about when you are pushed for time? Being too cognitively busy or physically exhausted is something that Daniel Kahneman talks about in his book *Thinking, Fast and Slow* (2011). At times like this, he says that our self-control is impaired and we can make dreadful decisions and even act out of character.

I think we can all relate to acting out of character when we are depleted, can't we? Sadly, we tend to make excuses for our lousy decisions and try to carry on. But wouldn't it be better if we recognised when we are too mentally and physically tired and simply put off making a decision until the next morning when we are less likely to make a mistake? Or perhaps talk things through with someone else if you have to make a quick decision or send a delicate email. They may help you think more clearly.

Gut feelings – can the body inform decision making?

Isn't it interesting how often we hear either 'first impressions count', meaning we should be paying attention to implicit (automatic) thinking, a gut feel; or conversely, 'putting first impressions aside', meaning gut feelings are notoriously unreliable, so we should solve problems with logic and relevant strategies. But according to Kihlstrom, an eminent professor of psychology, intuitions can be rational guides and therefore signals like a gut feel should not be ignored (2010).

In the previous chapter, Becoming exceedingly valuable: Problem solving and creative thinking, we discussed intuition, using the example of the senior fire officer who instinctively knew his men were in danger while combatting a fire in an industrial building. Psychologist Gary Klein's research looked at decision making by people working in the field and noted that intuition developed by experts displayed reliable and fast decision-making practices within their world of expertise, such as the behaviour of smoke at a fire scene, which involved pattern recognition below conscious awareness. At the time, Kahneman doubted the efficacy of intuition, but his research studied a different type of person, i.e. people who didn't have the opportunity to establish strong patterns in their work. Both researchers agree, however, that intuition is pre-conscious pattern recognition, therefore clearly involving memory. Consequently, intuition is learnt and will continue to develop in the right environment.

Gut feelings are different from intuition as they also have a physiological explanation. The gut (digestive system) is popularly known as your second brain. It can influence your emotions, immune system and your health. The gut functions without any input from the brain, and it is the only organ that can do this. The gut has over 100 million brain cells (neurons) and has its own nervous system, called the enteric nervous system. And it sends emotional signals *to* the brain, meaning that we feel with our gut before our brain knows. This information is relayed by the incredibly large vagus nerve that runs from the bottom of the digestive system all the way up to the cerebellum at the base of the brain.

Equally, information runs down from the brain to the gut with messages of peace or fight or flight. I'm sure you have felt many times how a big presentation can make you feel nervous in your stomach, as if under threat. This is the vagus nerve at work.

Decisions made by gut feeling tend to be those that you need to make quickly and which rely on unconscious processing, whereas when you have more time, you consciously and deliberately look at things logically.

In addition to this, and according to Damasio's somatic marker hypothesis, our memory of events associated with bodily sensations allows us to feel those sensations again. This in turn helps us decide what to do in similar situations. Bodily sensations and emotions are like a database that, once rapidly scrolled through, allows us to make a fast decision, a decision that could adversely affect our work and is urgent.

Gut feelings allow us to make decisions rapidly below conscious awareness by providing bodily feedback. This is highly useful in an urgent situation, especially considering the cacophony of stimuli bombarding us at any one time and competing for our attention. Good decision making is often physical. If you have time, however, and to cover all bases, perhaps it's wise to listen to those gut feelings, weigh up the information you have so far, and be aware of cognitive biases so that you feel more secure in your decision.

A word about customers and clients making decisions

These days, our customers and clients often know more about a company's services and products than its own employees because of the sheer breadth of online resources which freely display product descriptions, various professional and user reviews and more. This can be a problem when you are trying to change the patterns of thinking in the decision makers you are hoping to do business with.

One of the biggest mistakes people make when trying to influence the decisions of other people is to push too hard. People don't like to be pushed. They tend to dig their heels in and resist, regardless of their better judgement, and treat you with suspicion, thereafter damaging any future communication with you. It is far better to gently offer evidence, stories, anecdotes and statistics to allow the person to feel they are making their own mind up.

Bear in mind also, that if you are potentially a new supplier, the customer will want to stay with the company they know and will feel uncomfortable making a decision to change to your products. You will need to establish credibility in this instance. Perhaps you use your products yourself. Perhaps you know people they trust who use your services. Build up a persuasive case for them to decide to try something new with you.

In summary

In light of the evidence so far, to be good at making decisions it's wise to be aware that the majority of people use emotions to make decisions, even below conscious awareness. If you are to be able to influence people with integrity you need to take this into account. Equally, when you make a decision yourself, think of this to help you too. And, if it's an important decision, cross-reference with the logical way of looking at things and take your time to avoid heuristics and biases. If that's too complicated or time is too short, remember your gut, what is that telling you?

Action steps: how to create a decision-making environment

1. Learn to harness and appreciate your emotions. They are a barometer, a guide to help you make decisions. But be careful not to actually be emotional.

2. What is your working environment like? Is it light, airy, the right temperature, plants, fish in tanks? If not, can you change it? If it can't be enhanced, try having meetings outside, walking and talking.

3. Consider unconscious biases. You will have them, so try to identify them. Are you aware of looking for confirmation and ignoring falsifying evidence? Be brutally honest with yourself before making that decision.

4. Loss aversion may be one bias. Do you detect that within yourself?

5. Think of Sam at the beginning of this chapter. Sam put forward a logical case but it was not enough. Find out the emotional needs from your decision makers. Either meet those needs directly or engage them in conversation to influence them onto a different emotional path. But always have your logical case too.

6. When going into meetings, try to arrange them when people feel fresh and sated; they will be in a far more positive and agreeable mood.

7. Try not to make decisions when you are overwhelmed and exhausted either physically or mentally. Instead, make a note of how you think you would like to decide in that moment and then review your note in the morning. You may be surprised how close you came to making a mistake.

Chapter 6
**Enhancing your
communication skills
Fun**

Chapter 6
Enhancing your communication skills
Fun

Have you ever wondered why business meetings can be stressful, dull or ineffective? If we start a meeting in a negative brain state, we will not be very efficient at problem solving nor terribly creative at coming up with solutions. In fact, it is highly likely that whatever is decided, few of the meeting participants will implement any of the suggestions, meaning that the meeting was a waste of time. If, however, you start the meeting in a positive, fun way, this can all change for the better.

As mentioned in the introduction, when we put our brain in a pleasurable state we are the most efficient and effective we can be. Remember that although your brain is boss, it is up to you to control the state you wish to be in for your wellbeing and the wellbeing of those around you. Your customers, clients and colleagues will feel far more loyal to you and your brand when they are enjoying themselves. As the human brain evolved, the capacity for laughter preceded the capacity for speech. This is big news that you can use to influence even the most dire situations.

Why fun in business works so well

When I left school, the only thing I wanted to do was travel and have adventures. In those days, 'gap years' when students went away travelling were unheard of, at least in my world. With what I perceived to be limited options, I began working as a long-haul air stewardess with a major airline.

A few months into the job I was having a ball and loving every minute. I thought 'This is as good as it gets'. How wrong could I be? There was much more fun to come.

I was at London Heathrow Airport at the start of a two-week Caribbean trip. I boarded the aeroplane and began doing my pre-passenger checks with the rest of the crew. The girl looking after the first-class passengers held the position colloquially known as 'A' Bird. She was preparing the cabin and was busy opening the overhead lockers when one of them stuck and wouldn't open. The captain was standing close by in the doorway of the flight deck with his shiny four stripes on each shoulder of his jacket, hat with gold braid resembling scrambled egg and a cup of tea in one hand. The 'A' Bird said, 'Excuse me, Captain, would you mind helping me open this overhead locker please?'

'Sure,' he said, and with tea in one hand, he used the other to open the latch. As he did so, a large arm came swooping down towards him from inside the locker, holding out a hand to shake, with a voice saying, 'Hello, sir, my name is John Smith and I am your purser for this trip.'

With that, the captain's cup of tea flew in the air, splashing all over his immaculate hat and jacket, and with tea dripping from his nose, his trembling voice said, 'You *@!*. I will get you for this!' He was so shaken up, the first officer had to do the take-off.

To this day, I don't know how the averagely built John Smith was able to hide in the overhead locker, but hide he did. In fact, while John was still up there I went to see what all the ruckus was about, as the hooting and hollering was deafening. I looked up at where they were all pointing. At first, all I could make out was what looked like a coconut and some clothes. But as my eyes adjusted, I could see that the coconut was the top of John's head (he was slightly bald) and the clothes were the uniform he was wearing. The 'A' Bird was leaning on a seat laughing hysterically, the first officer and flight engineer were rolling around the flight deck with tears streaming down their faces, and the attending ground staff could hardly breathe. And so the laughter began on this particular flight assignment.

Clearly the 'A' Bird was in on the joke, but we all knew that any one of us could be involved in the next practical joke. To say we became vigilant is an understatement. But what we didn't expect was John playing tricks on the passengers as well.

Do you remember the safety announcement just before take-off? In those days, it was announced by a cabin crew member on a microphone at the front of the aeroplane. It's the long announcement about lifejackets, oxygen masks and brace positions in an emergency landing. As usual, only a few people were listening properly when it got to the part that says 'if in the unlikely event this aircraft should land on *water*...' It was at this point that John picked up another PA microphone in the rear galley, lowered it near the sink and turned the tap on so that along with the announcer's words was the sound of running water *inside* the cabin. The passengers were looking frantically forwards, backwards, upwards and downwards. They didn't know whether to laugh or cry. Thankfully, it was the former.

The passengers were suddenly alert to any other announce-ments with eyes wide, waiting in anticipation of the next trick. They were relishing the camaraderie and the feeling of being 'in on the jokes'. We fast became a single unit of fun and adventure, and even nervous passengers felt a sense of relief from tension and their fears seemed to melt away.

They weren't disappointed. Once we were airborne and later in the flight, things settled down and we had become lulled by the routine of looking after the passengers, when out of the corner of my eye I saw something unfamiliar. These same passengers were staring incredulously at the 'A' Bird, who had appeared, lying on her back on a trolley covered in paper towels that were splashed with tomato ketchup, holding a knife to her chest. With her eyes closed pretending to be dead, John wheeled her through the cabin.

Were the passengers cross or upset about all these antics? No, they loved every minute. We all did. In fact, after the two-week trip of fun and games, we got home to a suitcase full of complimentary letters.

I'm sure these extreme events wouldn't happen on an airline in this day and age, but I do sometimes wonder whether this is a good thing or not. You see, this is one of the best examples of superb customer service and employee engagement I have been personally involved in. We had fun, we stayed a strong team and the passengers were enthralled. There is no doubt that we secured customer loyalty and I am certain that those passengers became a superb onward sales team for the airline, telling everyone who crossed their path what a brilliant time they had.

So what is going on here? What is going on in the brains of the crew and the passengers? Why is fun and humour so important in business?

Fun and humour play a major part in our cognitive function. They help facilitate social engagement, which is vital for human survival. A network of cortical and subcortical structures in the brain are involved in processing the surprising incongruity that leads to laughter. These areas include the temporo-occipito-parietal regions. Add to this the structures in the brain which are involved in reward, attention and memory, and it shows that a lot of brain is at work when we are having so much fun.

When we laugh together we come together.

When we laugh together, we come together on common ground. Therefore, team building, interaction and social functions thrive. Think of a time when you found something funny and had fun – did stress, tension and fear diminish? This indicates that the stress hormone cortisol was inhibited. In different adverse circumstances, cortisol is likely to be secreted in abundance and will negatively affect our memory and blood pressure and could cause other physical problems too.

Go back to your personal example of experiencing fun. Were any feelings of tension replaced by a feeling of enthusiasm, energy and clear thinking? If so, the neurochemicals dopamine – which helps us feel motivated and reward driven – and serotonin – that regulates our mood, sleep, appetite and emotions – would have been working beautifully. This is quite a package to increase productivity, morale and camaraderie. Also when we feel less inhibited, we are far more likely to be innovative and forward thinking. A must for all business.

When the brain is in a pleasurable state it is effective and efficient.

Caveat

We have to be careful with humour, however. It doesn't always carry well across different cultures. For instance, some people find sarcasm or even humiliation to be funny. This is dangerous ground and can alienate people and have a negative effect. So be mindful of how others may perceive your comments. The point, however, is not to tell jokes badly or upset anyone, but to put people's brains in a pleasurable state for maximum effectiveness.

Equally, some people use humour to deflect their incompetence, so be careful of the person who uses humour and fun when it's inappropriate or who tirelessly acts like the clown. People like this will need managing carefully. Keeping things in perspective is wise.

Improving engagement and thinking clearly

Customer service, customer loyalty and customer engagement are a constant focus for most businesses. Equally, a high level of employee engagement saves enterprises and companies billions every year. When we can get these areas right, business has a far greater chance of succeeding. But you don't need me to tell you that. What is useful for you to know are ways to improve on engagement right across the board.

Speaking of the board...

How many times do you go into a board meeting, or any kind of business meeting for that matter, and grab a coffee, a sugary snack, sit down, check your phone again, wait for everyone to arrive, perhaps a bit of small talk, have a minor moan about something and then the last person comes rushing in and the meeting starts? The chair of the meeting launches straight into what the problem is that needs solving. He or she wants to be efficient and get on with it, because there is so much to do and waffle in meetings drives them mad.

> **If you are tense try to avoid sugary snacks and caffeine – they can fog your thinking.**

You are all expected to come up with a solution quickly and move on. But instead, tension is a little high, there is a bit of blaming, a couple of disagreements, and the odd person who says nothing and whose mind is probably elsewhere and thinking of something totally unrelated.

Solutions to the business issues may be found but not all meeting participants will truly be in agreement and, in effect, little is actually put into practice or achieved once outside the meeting room.

Now picture a scenario where you have planned an upbeat start to the meeting so that your colleagues are fully engaged before getting down to the nitty-gritty business. For instance, have each person update the rest on something they have succeeded in doing. It doesn't matter how small, what matters is that you put everyone in a positive mental state. Not showing off, not trying to look big, but simply and briefly talking about a good thing. Can you see how much more creative everyone will be when moving on to discuss the business issue that needs solving? Can you see how more people are likely to contribute to the solution, thus taking *ownership* and being more inclined to take the information and *do* something about it? A leader who achieves this is positively inspirational to work with.

> **Start each meeting with an update from everyone that is humorous or upbeat for creative thinking, cohesion and actions.**

Creative thinking, cohesion and actions are the result of putting everyone in a positive mental state at the beginning of meetings. And if you can get everyone laughing, all the better. Laughter is contagious; it only takes one person to start.

I thought long and hard about giving a whole chapter to the benefits of communicating well using fun, as I wondered if you might think this too frivolous and stop reading. But I wanted to demonstrate that putting you in a positive mental state at the outset of this chapter with the airline stories is the best way to engage you and prepare you for more information to come. I hope I succeeded.

Is it time to celebrate yet?

If you have managed to have some fun while working, the chances are you will be more successful. What do you do about those successes? Do you stop and savour the moment? Or do you rush to get the next job on your to-do list done? Isn't it a shame that we tend to ricochet from one task to the next, only thinking of how much there is left to do and how little time there is to get those things done. Sadly, it's the norm and there is certainly no fun in that.

It's always time to celebrate.

If you just take a moment to *stop* and savour the moment, that delicious feeling of doing well, of satisfying a customer or client, and of achievement will boost the feel-good neurotransmitters again, so that you are even more motivated to carry on. Or better still, why not become a child again and buy everyone an ice cream or cakes? It doesn't have to be very much at all, but, interestingly, sharing food offers an extra bonus. Research shows that when we share food with others we encourage reciprocation, which elevates our social relationship with them.

Now I'm not suggesting that you become best friends with everyone at work or even with your customers and clients, that would be quite ghastly in some situations. But what I am suggesting is that you consider social sharing in order to encourage professional cooperation. People naturally want to cooperate with those with whom they feel a social bond. It's a highly ethical way to influence others with integrity.

Therefore, not only will you be celebrating your successes to encourage your own continued motivation, but you will also be bonding with those around you. This bonding releases a rather delicious hormone in the brain called oxytocin, popularly known as the love hormone. It is secreted in abundance when a woman gives birth, and the more she hugs her baby, the more oxytocin she will produce. And it's cumulative: the more oxytocin she produces, the more she will hug her baby. This mechanism ensures mother and baby bonding. But oxytocin is relevant and highly useful to mention in a business context because it will ensure stronger business relationships when stimulated, even in small amounts, via social sharing. What better way to do this than through sharing food and celebrating business success?

> **Celebrating together will boost working relationships.**

Your people might be having an affair

What if, to-date, you have not been proactive in encouraging bonding and cooperation at work? Perhaps you have not encouraged opportunities to chat about things in general. If so, the chances are that you are not very likely to know whether your staff, customers or clients are happy with what you do.

For instance, are you aware of any discontent and whether your people or colleagues are looking for another job? Do you ask them all? Realistically, this is quite unlikely. I am sure you know about a few key people and the importance of getting to know your direct reports and colleagues, so that you understand them better, find out about their dreams and aspirations, in order to help them develop and grow. What better way to ensure they stay and remain committed to the company? But what about all the rest? How can you tell if they are content or happy with your efforts?

To ensure the majority of people around you are in the most effective state is to have fun anyway. Pre-empt any possible negativities rumbling in the background by lightening up, while at the same time promoting efficiency and success. Of course, for real grievances this will not be enough and you will need to meet these head on and do something about them immediately.

But fostering a culture which makes time and space to have fun as well as succeed in business will certainly iron out wrinkles of discontent. In fact, this is one of those tips that you can use in your personal life. Most relationships, whether at work or in your personal life, will not always go smoothly, so laughing together is such a great way to smooth out the pot holes in your journey together.

Sometimes, however, things still go wrong.

Demonising

I interviewed a holiday resort director a while ago. Naturally, a large percentage of his staff were customer facing. There was a great team spirit and they worked well together, enjoying their jobs and giving excellent service. He explained that one day a particularly grumpy guest was giving his team a hard time. This guest would click his fingers to get their attention, complain and was constantly rude. However hard they tried, they could not please this chap. In fact, he was so unkind he even managed to reduce one of the team members to tears.

Gradually, the boss became more and more agitated and started to pick fault in his people out of sheer frustration and temper. Team morale fell as increasingly they couldn't seem to do anything right.

Two things happened.

First the poison spread and affected the whole team and the boss to the point where other guests noticed. In fact, complaining began to build up a momentum of its own. Some complaints were justified because they were not now working so well as a team. Some, however, were not, but displaying true crowd behaviour, several people lost their sense of individuality and followed the emotions of the crowd, or in this case fellow guests.

Avoid crowd behaviour at all costs unless it supports your purpose.

Even those who managed to remain distant from the crowd still had that look in their eye that read 'there's no smoke without fire' and assumed that there must be something fundamentally wrong with their service if so much negativity was anything to go by.

Negativity bred negativity and the downward spiral was crystal clear as the reputation of the holiday resort dipped. And we all know how hard it is to build a good reputation and how amazingly quickly our reputation can come tumbling down.

That is, until the second thing happened.

One of the team members took a stand. He stopped following his own team's negativity and broke the simmering bubble of discontent that both customers and team were feeding. He made everyone laugh! One incredibly witty comment and everyone melted.

> **A suitable witty remark can save a company's reputation.**

His comment was respectful and relevant and he managed to turn a dreadful situation into something upbeat and fun. From that moment, the team picked up their enjoyment of working for the customers again and the customers enjoyed their efforts.

What happened to the original grumpy guest? Well, he went very quiet and they even managed to make him smile. Well, just a little...

The moral of this story – positive emotion saved the day. *However...*

On the other side of the coin. The customer who started the rot galvanised the other customers into a mini war through his overt negativity. You see, when we misunderstand people, when we don't communicate properly and when people make us feel bad, we begin to distance ourselves and even make up stories in our heads as to why they are not good people.

We actually demonise people who are 'not in our tribe'.

This is because human beings have an unfortunate habit of classifying people in one of two categories: 'friend', whom we go towards, or 'foe', whom we try to get away from. This is obviously to help us keep safe and recognise danger or threat. When we decide someone is a friend, our brains react in a similar way to theirs when we think of our own experiences. This provides greater opportunity to explore new ideas and bond.

If, however, we relegate people into the 'foe' box and subsequently demonise them, relationships can be destroyed and progress damaged. This is exceptionally bad for business. Ask yourself this question: have your customers ever demonised you? Or have you ever demonised others? Is your team split into a 'them' and 'us'?

The effect of both negative and positive emotion can be all-consuming and can hinder or stimulate creativity, learning and work performance and even mental and physical health. Emotion is a signal, a collection of information, as well as a barometer to pay attention to what is going on.

One of the best ways to navigate relationships within small teams or even larger companies is to adopt a culture of fun. Bonding and collaboration will result, thus enhancing creative thinking and people taking responsibility for their actions because they care about outcomes and their colleagues, customers and clients. Creating this kind of atmosphere will empower everyone to feel they are influential and in charge of their own destiny.

In the example that opened this chapter, it was a great feeling for my colleagues and me to positively influence all those passengers to believe in the airline that we as a team were working for. Everyone involved felt upbeat, well and on top of things.

Learning how to use feelings for your and everyone's advantage is the next step in this book. Enjoy.

Action steps: how to use fun to improve your communication skills

1. At the start of every meeting, put everyone in a positive mental state for optimum problem solving by asking each person to update the rest of the group on something that was fun, or even humorous, that happened to them recently.

2. Let it be known that this is the way all meetings will start from now on. It is likely that people will actively look for fun things that are going on in their lives to prepare. This will offer the added bonus of paying attention to the positives in one's life.

3. Celebrate your own and others' successes to boost morale. It doesn't have to be expensive – a round of ice creams will work.

4. Sharing food to celebrate will especially elevate social bonding, so perhaps provide some cakes next time.

5. The best leaders and colleagues have a sense of humour, know when to keep things light without sarcasm or humiliation.

6. We have little control of the bigger ghastly things that may happen, but we can control how we react to daily occurrences. If we lighten up and have fun, we can ride the big waves without drowning.

7. Highlight to everyone that having fun has health benefits and boosts business.

8. Communicating your ideas with fun will help people feel curious and want to explore ways of moving forward.

9. Choose smaller goals that can be achieved quickly to satisfy and promote the feel-good neurotransmitters which will encourage further achievements.

10. Consider how you might use fun every time you have a message to share.

Chapter 7
Boosting your message
Understanding and using feelings

Chapter 7
Boosting your message
Understanding and using feelings

If you meet with customers or clients with one goal in mind – how you want that person or people to feel at the end of the meeting – you will stay more actively engaged in what they are saying so that you can respond to their words in the moment rather than think of your own script.

Focusing on how you want them to feel will keep you on track more than any other goal. Equally, when you identify the core feelings you want your business to project, you will align all marketing material, conversations and the company mantra. Feelings are highly influential and can be harnessed to stay on message.

Emotions are different from feelings

In Chapter 6 we discussed how using fun in business can drive a high level of customer service and employee engagement. We also looked at the value of negative emotion. Emotion persuades, it engages and it makes things memorable.

The part of the brain that processes emotion is a primitive cognitive system which evolved primarily to appraise a situation. Emotions give meaning to the information about the outside world that your senses provide. If, for instance, your nose detects the smell of smoke, the emotion of fear will raise your heartbeat and prepare your muscles to run without you consciously having to do anything at all. This rapid response is what emotions are for. We have little control over this because the emotional response is automatic. Emotion is a response that is chemically and neurologically produced by the brain when presented with appropriate stimuli.

However, after an automatic emotional response, we become conscious of the emotional experience. Once we are consciously aware of our emotional experience we react accordingly. For instance, as soon as you realise that the smell of smoke is simply burnt toast you can laugh at yourself for having grabbed your mobile phone and rushed out of the door.

The area of the brain associated with emotional processing is the limbic system, but there are also other smaller emotional systems which sub-serve different emotions; for instance, the insula is associated with the emotion 'disgust'. It is relevant to know that there are various systems in the brain for processing emotion because it highlights the far-reaching dynamics and relationships with other areas of the brain.

The emotional part of the brain, the limbic system, is the original boss and the decision maker. It took us a long time in our evolution for the prefrontal cortex (PFC) area of the brain to evolve for higher-order processing. Generally, people think that because the PFC is responsible for higher-order processing it must be the new boss, but it is not as in charge as we like to believe. (Chapter 5 goes into far more detail about decision making.)

On the other hand, according to Damasio (2000), feelings are different from emotions in that they are our own private mental picture, made up of our perceptions of the physical reactions of the emotions. Feelings amplify the impact of emotions and are associated with meaning, with higher cortical systems being involved. Feelings are intimate and often others are not aware of what someone else is feeling.

> **Feelings amplify the impact of emotions, and provide us with more meaning.**

We tend to show our emotions, but we rarely show our intimate feelings. This is a useful point to remember in business. We are more likely to understand someone's emotional journey when we are trying to help them in a business sense, but to detect how someone actually feels is far more difficult.

Imagine, for instance, you are selling the benefits of an advisory service you provide. Perhaps you are a financial adviser and you are talking to an elderly potential client. Of course, you will ask lots of questions to find out what they want to do with their money. They will probably tell you about their children and grandchildren, perhaps how they would like to help their grandchildren get on the property ladder or clear university debts or to take them on a holiday. Once you have found out what their wishes are, you can take them on an emotional journey to help them make the best financial choices specific to their circumstances. This is an enjoyable task, but it takes practice.

However, to take this conversation to the next level you need to understand that you are not necessarily aware of how this person is feeling. Perhaps they don't themselves recognise what their feelings mean. Do they feel uneasy, but put on a brave face and assume their uneasy feeling is because they are discussing money – which they perhaps dislike doing? Or even worse, might they think they are feeling uneasy because they don't like you? In actual fact, the uncomfortable feeling might be because, in truth, they would rather spend the money on buying a new boiler and having their kitchen refitted, but they feel guilty about it. Or maybe they are feeling angry and hurt because they don't see their grandchildren very often and would actually prefer not to give them any money but feel they should.

We may show our emotions but we rarely show our feelings.

So how can you handle this? It is tempting for me at this point to suggest ways of detecting feelings, but I think this is both dangerous and unnecessary. You are a business person and I am sure you would prefer to focus on business and not on being a pseudo-psychologist. But it is important to be aware that feelings and emotions can make or break a business transaction, a relationship and most forms of communication.

In a business environment, the best way to detect if there is dissonance between the emotional signals someone is revealing and how they are actually feeling is to give them your complete attention. This is difficult, because there is always a profusion of stimuli competing for our attention at any one time. Also, the selective processing of the emotional significance of stimuli has an evolutionary advantage, as we are wired for positive and negative emotion to modulate pleasure-seeking and defensive behaviour, to ultimately lead to reproduction or survival. It's tough to override that! As such, only a fleeting glimpse of an emotionally relevant cue from another person is sufficient to reach our own awareness and perception. And it is this that you can work with.

As you can see, there is a distinction between emotion and feelings even though they work together. When we understand the interaction between them, we are able to be more objective in assigning meaning to emotion and stand back to evaluate what is going on. A strong position to hold. This ability is highly useful both in business and your private life.

Working with feelings

There is an unspoken assumption that serious business people have little need to consider feelings. Unless you are in the advertising industry, which has long put feelings at the centre of a campaign – such as stimulating the feelings of being an idyllic, perfect family while buying confectionery or feeling like a wonderful mother because of a washing-up liquid – the rest of the business world rarely puts feelings high on the agenda.

What a dreadful waste of an excellent resource.

Perhaps you, as a modern business person, may already consider ethically influencing others by using feelings to be part of your business development plan and recognise that honing this resource is part of your transferable skills portfolio. Nevertheless, it is useful to understand fully not only how valuable feelings are in business, but also how different they are from emotions and how best to be aware of and work with feelings with your customers, clients and colleagues to everyone's advantage.

In order for you to create your own system for using feelings as part of your business skill set, this chapter offers three areas for you to consider:

1. How to use feelings to motivate and influence.
2. Being aware of how you want people to feel at the end of meetings to ensure greater focus, engagement and understanding.
3. Finding a unique feeling that your company would find beneficial to achieve, which can become the core ethos for clarity and understanding.

First, let's begin with this unique case study.

Case study: Dr An Wang

Back in the 1950s, a Chinese immigrant to the United States called Dr An Wang founded a small engineering company. One of Dr Wang's inventions, magnetic core memory, became a foundation block in the emergence of computers. To sustain and grow his small start-up company, Dr Wang sold the patent for magnetic core memory to the giant corporation IBM for $500,000, quite a substantial sum at that time. With the proceeds of this transaction, he founded a company bearing his own name, Wang Laboratories Inc., which grew to become one of IBM's biggest competitors.

There is something terrific about working with founders of companies. They are passionate about their baby, they want to see it develop and grow, be healthy and watch employees take pride in their creation.

In so doing, Dr Wang succeeded handsomely. By the 1980s, business was booming, Wang Laboratories Inc. had grown to over 30,000 staff around the world and times were great. Everyone was making plenty of money and they were enjoying the culture of the company. All was good.

Year after year I went to Wang's annual sales achiever conferences. My husband was Wang Achiever and as an outsider I watched these testosterone-charged events with great interest.

Things took a turn for the worse when Dr Wang was forced to stand down as president of the company due to throat cancer.

At the subsequent achiever conference event we attended, as usual there were very few saleswomen so the conference room was typically bursting at the seams with success-driven men who arguably in those days didn't have such a thing as a feminine side to get in touch with. There was nothing these guys hadn't heard before in business; they had been around the block many times. But with the patriarch absent as a result of his serious health problem and some dubious strategic decisions having been taken by the company during his absence, results had dipped and morale was slipping. These top salespeople knew that the company was in trouble and many were looking for new jobs, and basically jumping ship while the going was good.

The atmosphere at the conference was one of unrest and aggression, with inflated egos and a dog-eat-dog attitude. Suddenly, without any prior indication, Dr Wang made an appearance on the stage to speak. No one expected to see him because of his fight against throat cancer and he was very unwell. The room fell silent as he began his short speech with a gravelly, hoarse voice. He told everyone how proud he was of what they had all created together. He thanked everyone for making Wang Laboratories Inc. such a wonderful place to work. He addressed the fact that things weren't good. He then asked if they would please help him to make the company great again. His closing words were 'will you help me?'

In just a few short minutes Dr Wang had reduced hundreds of antagonistic baying hounds and doubters into a single roaring body of acclaim, with damp-eyed men giving him the standing ovation of their lives. There truly wasn't a dry eye in the house.

Dr Wang succeeded in persuading people to stay with the company and galvanised their support like I had never seen. It was a remarkable speech and it was all based on how he made people feel.

The Dr Wang example shows that he deliberately and success-fully managed to persuade the audience to make the decision to support him and the company by using an emotionally charged speech not only to stimulate an emotional response but to arouse deep feelings, as evidenced by the standing ova-tion and tears. You may be thinking this was a cheap shot, using his health to turn the company around. But this doesn't detract from the fact that the way he made people feel did more in those few minutes than any other form of communication.

Feelings to motivate and influence

So how does this relate to your scenario? How can you use this case study and apply it to your own situation? It is unlikely that you are the leader of a massive company that is going through hard times and you are unwell, but the principles are the same for everyone.

Take, for instance, a managing director I worked with. He was almost out of his mind with worry about a shareholder meeting he had the next day. The news he had to deliver wasn't good and he knew he would be in for a gruelling time. He felt he had to put a veneer on a presentation purely based on spreadsheets and the negative statistics. His face etched with worry, it was clear they would smell the fear and make his day a misery.

As he told me his story he became animated and warm as he recounted his love of the business. His sincerity, authenticity and hard-work ethic shone as he recounted stories of his enthusiastic and loyal staff. The hard lines on his face softened and one couldn't help but feel this man needed support, not a beating.

Yes, he evoked all those feelings in me and I knew he could do the same with the shareholders, so my suggestion was to go into the meeting showing the emotions that he had shown me and only then offer the figures and statistics. So that is what he did. The shareholders were moved by the feelings he instilled in them and it worked. He was one relieved man and the worry melted away as they agreed to give him the time and support he needed to turn things around.

In another instance, I told the Dr Wang story to a man who had just sold his small garden centre business. The new owners wanted him to stay on as manager for the next year, as is quite normal. But he now had to manage in the way that the new owners wanted and not the way he was used to. The stress was palpable and he looked exhausted. I suggested he simply took his staff to the local pub and follow the Dr Wang model by explaining how he was feeling and simply asking for their help. His small speech wasn't going to win any speaker prizes, but he succeeded in changing how the people felt and they were happy to support him in his final year in the business.

How do you want people to feel when they leave your meeting?

Have you ever considered how you want people to feel once they have finished their meeting with you?

This is one of the most effective approaches and skills to develop. Before any kind of meeting, ask yourself how you want that person or people to feel. Do you want them to trust you, to feel safe, to feel significant? What is the most beneficial feeling you can induce to facilitate better understanding and communication?

For instance, if you are in the health industry perhaps you want people to feel *energised* after meeting you or feel *inspired* to buy a new membership. If this is the case, then focus on your meeting being upbeat and energetic or motivate them by finding out what they want to achieve and showing them how to attain those aspirations with your help.

Or perhaps you run a funeral business (no link, I promise!). When you meet clients you will probably want to help them feel looked after and comfortable that you will take care of all the arrangements so that they have less to worry about. The bereaved find it hard to think clearly, partly because they are often in shock, so they will want to *trust* you to take care of everything and to carry out any specific wishes they may have.

The situation is different when speaking to your staff at the funeral business, as you will want them to feel confident yet upbeat in their work. They face a difficult job and it will do no one any favours if they feel down all the time. So if you notice that morale is low, perhaps your meeting with them could focus on helping them feel *proud* of their professionalism when helping those who are suffering.

Setting aside a few minutes when preparing for each meeting to think about how you want your people to feel at the end of it will keep you in the present moment and really concentrating on them in order to achieve the desired outcome, which is to have them in the most helpful and productive state possible when getting back down to their work.

Generally, in meetings or discussions our attention span is notoriously limited and it can be difficult to maintain focus on someone when you have messages to deliver yourself. There is nothing worse than directing your concentration on waiting for someone else to stop talking so that you can dive in with what you want to say, regardless of the information they have just given you. Vital clues can easily be missed. However, if during the conversation you have in the back of your mind how you want them to feel by the end of the session, you will engage far better. You are much more likely to pick up any dissonance between what they are saying and what they are feeling because you will detect a fleeting look or flicker of the eye, and you will be able to change the course of the discussion to probe a little deeper and find out what is really going on. And the great thing is, you don't need a script, because you will be listening with far more acuity and answering accordingly, gently steering the conversation and actions as needed to help shareholders, colleagues, customers, clients, family and friends or anyone to feel the most benefit at that moment.

Focusing on how you want people to feel during a meeting keeps you engaged.

This is an excellent and transferable business skill.

The importance of knowing what the core feeling of your business is

A lot of companies have created 'mission statements' and sometimes also 'core values', but these often ignore feelings and emotion and it is difficult for employees and customers to relate to and benefit from mission statements like 'to be the No 1 or No 2 vendor in three out of our five chosen markets globally'. These statements therefore don't actually achieve as much as they could.

If, however, you consider emotion and how you want various stakeholders, especially customers, to feel, establishing a core feeling for the business can be far more powerful and of greater value in day-to-day activities. That said, this needs to be thought about carefully as there is no point in trying to influence how people feel about a company or product if this is not in keeping with its market positioning or priorities. There are many facets of the business that a company might take seriously. For instance, health and safety is extremely important for roller-coaster rides, so if you owned a roller-coaster park, you might think that safety is an important feeling to convey to your customers. But for the customer, this is a secondary consideration, because what the customer is buying is the feeling of exhilaration and excitement. For best results therefore, you would advertise your rides as hair-raising and fun. This is what people will buy and is the core feeling of the business that should be instilled in the behaviours of the staff. Of course, your reputation needs to be reliable and safe as well, through solid health and safety procedures and internal training, but this isn't the core feeling that will sell tickets and send customers home happy and recommending your business to family and friends.

A practical exercise

This is an exercise that can work very well with a group of people around the table. Investigating and establishing these core feelings will lead to clarity and cohesion in moving forward, so it's worth spending time to work it out if you're not absolutely clear already.

This is how to achieve the best results.

Ask these questions of the group:

- How does our company want people to feel about our products?
- What is the feeling we wish to evoke in order for people to buy?

List all the words you can think of as relevant to how people can feel. See Figure 1 below for some ideas.

Happy	Confident	Nurtured	Proud	Frugal
Important	Childlike	Secure	Pampered	Responsible
Kind	Strong	Wise	Clever	Loving
Trusted	Trustworthy	Significant	Healthy	Admiration
Wealthy	Patriotic	Efficient	Support	

Figure 1: Examples of feelings you might wish to evoke in customers

Brainstorm a variety of words initially, but then use the rest of the time to settle on the most appropriate feeling you want to create. Try to agree on one word, one feeling you wish to evoke.

This most appropriate core feeling you want your business to project can help frame all sales, marketing, advertising and any communication for the better. Your company bespoke feeling can become the company mantra, a core value that can be on all signature blocks and on posters around the office walls. There are many ways to keep this in mind when working on a daily basis to better ensure cohesion and focus. I have observed that when companies do this and they stay true to this core message, all employees understand better what needs to be done on every call or communication to stay on track, and clients and customers feel they understand your business better too. Such consistency and clarity leads to stronger businesses.

Identify the core feeling you want your business to project and use it as your company mantra.

Feelings are often thought to be abstract, to have no place in business or are not even considered. But in actual fact, when understood and ingrained they empower business and people.

Action steps: how to use feelings to boost your message

1. If you feel passionate about work, show it. It will increase loyalty and motivation.
2. Have regular meetings with colleagues and staff, and keep everyone up to date even if the news is not so good.
3. Before each meeting, take a few minutes to work out how you want the person or people to feel when the meeting is over. This will aid awareness and understanding.
4. No matter how many staff you have working for you, the same rule applies: how do you want them to feel at the end of each meeting? Work it out and stay on track. You will be far more influential.
5. Always consider what is the most helpful and productive state you can leave others in.

6. Work out your company or organisation's core message in terms of how you want your customers or clients to feel.

7. Once the core message has been established, tell all staff, print it on all communications, have posters around the walls with the one feeling you wish to convey.

8. Consider how you might specifically present this information to your prospective clients and existing customer base.

9. Think about how your company core values line up with those of your customers. Will you have to talk about this slightly differently with each one?

10. Can you use this information in your personal life?

11. Create two columns on a piece of paper. On one side, write down your organisation's core 'feeling'. On the other side, write down how you like to feel. Is there alignment? If there is, you are more likely to resonate with the company you are working for and feel happier.

12. Recognise when people need a break. Not only will this stop burnout, it will also show you care.

13. Acknowledge people's experience and knowledge, listen to them and take on board their views.

Chapter 8
The ultimate goal
Influence

Chapter 8
The ultimate goal
Influence

Psychological theories and neuroscience are contributing more and more to business research and will no doubt continue to do so for years to come. So far in this book we have looked at perception, cognition, emotion, health, behavioural skills and motivation so that you can tailor and target your goals and desires with greater accuracy, helping you to develop you and your business as well as those who work for you by building high-achieving teams of people to drive business forward.

You have read and devoured tips that will help you develop the characteristics of a strong manager to successfully scale up business and finely tune *your brain* to be the best *boss*. There is, however, one step left to achieve in order to become a person of influence. Someone who is the 'go-to' person to see clearly what needs to be done, a voice of reason and a 'safe pair of hands' when it comes to moving business forward.

This last step is to become trusted.

You will have already earned respect through having (hopefully) put some of the actions in place that were mentioned in the last seven chapters. It is now time to bring it all together.

Neuroscientific research shows that generosity, kindness and altruism are key to putting the brain in an optimum state. When this happens, stress levels diminish, the feel-good neurochemicals in your brain help you feel great and you become a magnet for positive outcomes. Once we achieve this we are healthier, wealthier and trusted by those we connect with. This is the ultimate goal for business to thrive and for you to become a trusted influencer that people look up to and rely upon, and it is the key to enjoying the power of recommendation.

Trust is truly the key to the power of reputation and recommendation.

Becoming influential – step one is altruism

A while ago I was on my way to a meeting in Fulham, London. I parked my car and walked through a small park to get to the street I needed. As I hurried along in my high heels concentrating on avoiding slipping on the fallen leaves, I noticed a rather dirty-looking man lying asleep on a bench. His long grey stained coat was covered in moisture from the autumn dew and he looked cold. I couldn't see his hands because he was huddled up trying to keep them warm. On the ground beside him were three carrier bags that looked as if they contained some old rags. I hurried past and kept walking out of the far side gate to reach my destination.

A while later, after my business meeting was over, I walked back through the park towards my parked car. The man was still there, he hadn't moved.

Again I kept walking. Just before passing through the gate to finally leave the park, I don't know why but I stopped. I turned round and retraced my steps past the sleeping man for a third time, went back out of the park and found a small supermarket. I bought a cheese sandwich and a carton of orange juice.

Yet again I entered the park. I very quietly approached the sleeping man. The last thing I wanted was for him to awake, startled. I gently put the food and drink by his head and carried on back to my car. That was it.

This was some years ago and I didn't talk about this for a very long time, but I do now to demonstrate a point. The valuable learning for me from this scenario was that I felt good for days after. I was on a roll. I was effective, efficient and happy. I was writing copy, delivering talks, my consultancy was going well, I could do no wrong. My work was going through the roof.

> **Altruism: doing something for someone else without expecting anything in return has an incredible effect.**

At the time, I was struck that as a result of trying to help someone, they had in fact helped me. Back then, I didn't know why I was on such a high, but when later I began to study neuroscience I thought about this story and wondered what went on in my brain.

And this is what I discovered. Imagine your typical working day. Some of the time, perhaps even most of the time, you are probably handling problems, irritating interruptions from time wasters or a whole host of annoying things stopping you from getting your to-do list done.

Stress alert! Under normal conditions, a certain amount of stress is a good thing. It keeps us on the ball; we are sharp and firing on all cylinders. Even the major stressful events in life such as bereavement, divorce or moving house will peak and dissipate over time. But it's the nagging, daily, seemingly inconsequential anxieties that cause the most harm. Through evolution, the onset of feeling stress and anxiety is meant to alert us to a possible threat to our survival, and it causes a narrowing of our focus to tackle the perceived threat. This means that when we are in a stressful state, our creativity, problem-solving and decision-making skills are adversely affected, which evidently is harmful in a working environment.

> **It's the nagging daily stress that causes most damage.**

Conversely, if we can put our brain into a pleasurable state we will be at our most efficient and effective because we are opening up our attention and ourselves for the very reason that we feel safe and therefore positive. This means that creativity and productivity are enhanced. (There is more detail on stress in Chapter 2.)

We have already talked about feel-good neurotransmitters in the brain in previous chapters, but there is another neuro-transmitter I would like to introduce here. This one is actually a neuro gas called nitric oxide (NO). It's released in little puffs, mostly from the lining of blood vessels. Because it is a gas it diffuses rapidly right through cell walls. NO increases circulation and is also a neuromodulator, increasing excitability (i.e. increasing neuronal firing rate) and increasing or decreasing neurotransmitter release. When NO is up, the stress hormone cortisol is down, feel-good serotonin increases and dopamine is regulated.

Don't you just love brains? So how do we get these glorious nitric oxide molecules? Exercise is an answer. When running or working out, the muscles need more oxygenated blood, NO is released in the lining of our arteries and this in turn widens the artery walls, enabling increased blood flow. As a vasodilator, it has long been used by the medical profession in the treatment of heart disease and strokes.

We can also increase NO with a healthy diet rich in the amino acids L-arginine and L-citrulline, meat, dairy, fruit and nuts, spinach and beetroot, as well as antioxidants such as vitamin C, garlic and so on. NO lasts for only a few seconds so it's important to maintain a healthy diet.

There is, however, quite a lot of interesting research that demonstrates a link between kindness, generosity and altruism and chemicals such as NO.

> **Kindness, generosity and altruism put the brain in the most effective state.**

NO is also a neuropeptide, a bi-directional tiny molecule of parts of proteins. Researchers such as Dawson and Snyder (1994) show that neuropeptides switch on emotion and emotion switches on neuropeptides. They are involved in hormone regulation, they help the body repair after injury, help with storing memories and support the immune system.

Specific neuropeptides like endorphins are natural painkillers. Another, oxytocin, lowers blood pressure and reduces stress and inflammation. And vasopressin and NO also increase circulation, which supports a healthy heart.

Neuropeptides also act as hormones, which means that they reach further than the brain and into the body. So when we get a gut feel about something, a receptor to neuropeptides in the gut tells us to listen to our apparent intuitions, which, according to Lieberman (2013), are in fact an emotional response from these tiny messengers.

And to add to this amazing merry dance, being generous and altruistic activates the mesolimbic reward pathway, which is an ancient part of the brain. This means that we are hardwired to be generous and kind.

There is an increasing amount of evidence from contributors such as Benson and colleagues (2007) that suggests that giving of ourselves and helping others may actually lengthen our lives and help us feel a whole lot better in the process. Whether or not altruism and kindness lead to longevity, the health benefits while we are alive are clear.

And as an added bonus away from the workings of our brains and bodies, when we seek to be of service to others, we naturally grow our social network, so that isolation and loneliness are a thing of the past. Our lives have more meaning when we give, so we feel valuable and valid. Our own problems are put into perspective, because if we focus our attention only on ourselves everything grows out of proportion as our view is so narrowed. But when we look outside ourselves, our problems don't seem so bad and we discover more chances to blossom and thrive.

> **Doing something for someone else helps us cope with our own problems better.**

Consequently, my kind act to the man sleeping on the park bench opened up a whole new way of thinking about the brain and wellbeing for me. I know that I didn't stimulate NO for three days, that's not how it works, but the knock-on effect was truly powerful in terms of how I felt and how efficient I was. From the evidence presented here, it is clear that there are benefits from asking ourselves what we can do to help others and, in so doing, we naturally help ourselves.

Caveat

But there is a caveat here. If we *constantly* seek ways to be generous and kind we can get a bit overwhelmed, which can be stressful in itself. In that case, let's not beat ourselves up about trying to be too angelic, we're only human, after all. We do need to be kind to ourselves as well.

There is also another point to make. When we are kind, some people will take advantage. As I'm sure you know, there are takers in the world who can be selfish and their attitude can be contagious. It doesn't seem to occur to them that they don't help others, but they are the first to accept a helping hand and let people do far too much for them. You are probably thinking of someone like this right now. It is an annoying and irritating trait and such people are not the sort of people you want in your team because negative attitudes are toxic. You can't blame others if they start to think 'why bother?'

If, however, you have encountered someone like this that you are trying to work with, have you tried talking to them? Perhaps you have pointed out the ethos of the group and how you all support one another. That may work, but, to be honest, it may not be blunt enough. It might not occur to them that they are not being supportive. Some people can't seem to connect ideals with actual behaviour, especially if it's their own!

I know a senior manager who had one such person in his team. Everyone was talking about him behind his back. Even the normally quiet ones were rising to the bait. The manager was fed up with how much time was being wasted on gossiping and he could see that productivity was down due to the low mood of most of his people. So he called the person into his office and decided to be more direct. 'I don't know if you're aware of this, but others are talking about you. They think you are happy to take assistance and they are becoming hacked off that you don't offer to help others. I know you are a great guy and are probably horrified to hear this, but I think you should know. How can we get over this?'

He was visibly shocked. 'No one has ever said that to me before. I didn't realise.'

Now, he could have reacted with anger, or with a 'so-what-do-I-care' attitude, but he actually liked his job and wanted to make things better. And that's what he did.

Philanthropy really does benefit more than those we are being kind to; it also benefits ourselves and business.

If we get something out of helping someone else does that mean there is no such thing as altruism?

Becoming influential – step two is trust

When we become more observant and notice opportunities to help others, we are likely to build new relationships. Relationships are one of the foundations of creating lasting change at work and in our personal lives.

From birth, the relationships we have with our parents, care givers and significant others mould who we are. During infancy, we are influenced by our environmental and social upbringing, and if this is healthy we have a greater chance of growing into emotionally well-balanced adults.

Equally, the plasticity of the brain is phenomenal and it will be modified by experiences and those around us. There is no age limit to this – we can improve and redirect our lives at any time. This is why it is important to build healthy relationships in order to rewire our neural functions so as to improve our cognitive abilities and also to enhance our emotional wellbeing.

And in the business world, more than ever we are realising that to achieve better sales, improve employee engagement, deliver great customer service and work with a team of high-functioning individuals who contribute brilliantly, we must focus on building effective professional relationships.

Good business is all about relationships.

This is about bonding.

Even the corporate world, where networking was not high on the agenda in past times, is now changing, with an increasing number of people spreading their net to gain more contacts. But of course, it's not just about collecting business cards, it's actually building relationships by offering to be of service to others, and to help them if you can.

This is also about trust. Trust makes people outstanding at work.

In Chapter 6 I have already mentioned a neurochemical called oxytocin, a hormone which acts as a neuromodulator. Scientist Dr David Hamilton has written widely on this subject.

As mentioned earlier, in the popular press, oxytocin has become known as the bonding chemical or love hormone. It's secreted in abundance when a woman gives birth and breast feeds, to aid mother and baby bonding. The more she feeds and hugs her baby, the more oxytocin she will produce and the more oxytocin she produces, the more she will feed and hug her baby. So we have this wonderful feedback loop in the brain.

There has been a lot of research into oxytocin which confirms that it enhances pro-social behaviour, one particular area being that of trust. Experiments show that when people feel trusted they produce more oxytocin in the brain. And the more oxytocin they produce, the more they become trustworthy. Yet again this displays a beneficial feedback loop. We actually become more trustworthy when we are trusted. And of course, the reward centres in the brain are activated too, thus supporting a positive attitude and greater wellbeing.

And to add to this delicious cocktail, when we trust someone else they trust us back, which leads to more secretions of oxytocin. This is excellent news because oxytocin is an anti-inflammatory and an antioxidant, so we feel better and may even look younger!

The important point to highlight is that science shows us that when we trust someone they become more trustworthy. Can you imagine how that can enhance your business relationships? Think of someone who works for you. They want to work from home two days a week and you are worried they will not be putting the same amount of effort in. If you trust them and resist micromanaging, which itself sends subliminal messages of distrust, they are very likely to become more trustworthy and work even harder than they would in the office. Of course, you will need to hold review sessions to make sure things are going according to plan, but if you have briefed them properly and they have the relevant resources, there is no reason why this shouldn't be a success. Unless, of course, your employee isn't up to the job, but the sooner you find this out, the better for everyone's benefit.

Remember, though, that company policies are often at the heart of the company's culture and attitude to trust. Therefore, it's necessary to make sure these policies are aligned with what leaders and employees wish for. If alignment is not achieved, nothing we can do or say will make any difference.

The need for flexibility at work is going to become more common as the needs of workers change and the costs of office space increase. Take, for instance, the rapidly growing section of society, the sandwich generation – people who have both children and elderly parents to look after. Tending to both generations, looking after your partner and the home and juggling work is highly stressful and can impact on work performance. Can you imagine a company that accommodates and supports this cohort?

This is not some utopian or Shangri-La place to work. Companies that consider these things not only exist right now, they are also thriving. More and more companies are adopting a positive attitude towards flexible working. Not only that, but staff on flexible working patterns regard this as a valuable benefit and often go that extra mile with more ideas for improvement, creative problem solving and commitment and loyalty to the firm.

I know one chap who has a child with special needs. His company supports him and gives him as much flexibility as he wants. This man knows he could get more money elsewhere, but the attitude of his company is more valuable to him than money. So he stays and gives 100 per cent at work. It is a myth that people are only motivated by money. You may be surprised if you ask what really drives people.

This boils down to flexible working, when people are trusted to work from home.

The more we trust someone, the more they become trustworthy.

A recent Gallup survey showed that 60–80 per cent of people think that working remotely is a positive development and boosts engagement. In fact, from research surveys it is estimated that 25 per cent of workers already believe that we are moving away from traditional working. The general consensus is that a major part of the workforce will be self-employed working a portfolio across multiple organisations. Furthermore, it is projected that over 20 per cent of the workforce will be consultants and temporary staff by 2022. Some companies are already preparing for this. Are you ready for such a shift?

Equally, we need to consider that office space is expensive and, quite frankly, often ugly or even dirty. Commuting is expensive and time consuming, and we are all required to consider our corporate social responsibility and think about environmental issues such as traffic pollution and fuel costs.

The future of success at work relies upon trust.

Top management can often be unaware of what's happening further down the organisational hierarchy, while uncertainty and a lack of trust are common amongst workforces in many parts of the world. Trust and honesty within your team is a must. Your staff need to have faith in you and the same applies to you having faith in your staff. Generally speaking, if you can trust your colleges and you are highly ethical, they will follow suit. After all, the success of any company is down to the combined efforts of all employees and not just the members on the board.

Having better staff relationships is also important to help those at the top feel less isolated metaphorically sitting in their ivory tower.

Another caveat

But there is another caveat here. Because oxytocin is associated with social memories, when a person we trust lets us down it is worse than if we hadn't trusted them at all in the first place. So be careful. If you are trusted by customers, clients or colleagues you must do everything in your power to maintain that trust. If you make a mistake, immediately put your hands up and say sorry! With luck and goodwill, if your apology is sincere and you can do something to fix the transgression, you may have a chance of patching up the relationship. But there are no guarantees, such is the power of oxytocin.

Becoming influential – step three is loyalty

From trust comes loyalty. In fact, I was speaking with a senior sales director who was unfaltering in his view that without loyalty we have no customers or clients. His thinking centred around the premise that just because someone buys from you once, this does not make them a customer or client. They should still be treated as a prospect until you are the only person they think of when they want the products you offer.

> **From trust comes loyalty.**

Thinking about it, he has a point. If someone buys from you once and you stop 'courting' them in the same way you did when starting the relationship, there is a good chance they will go to the next person who pursues them. If you truly want to achieve excellent relationships in business and to secure loyalty, it would seem you need to keep phoning, meeting and offering to help them where you can. Once you have built up trust and become the 'go-to' person, then that's an achievement worth talking about.

Becoming influential – collaboration, team spirit and individuality

Our digital world has erased boundaries and borders as we develop virtual collaboration. We have covered the importance of building strong relationships with our employees, endeavouring to find out what they think, what ideas they have, how they see the future in the industry and so on, the premise being that if the staff are happy then the customers and clients are far more likely to be happy. Great so far and clearly collaboration is a key to success.

What if, however, with our focus on collaboration and team work, we are not actually being as successful as we need? Is it possible we are losing sight of the advantages of being self-centred or egocentric? What if we are doing a disservice to the business leader who has little time for relationship building? After all, inventors, innovators and creative people are individuals who have original ideas and designs and are not, almost by definition, team players. Their thoughts are their own. They can certainly be tweaked by a team and implemented by colleagues, but only following the original idea.

Even in teams, individuals need to know the golden nugget 'what's in it for me?' (WIIFM), something team builders often overlook, where WIIFM can sometimes be seen as close to treason. But the truth is, however, that everyone needs to know how things may benefit them individually if they are to contribute to team success.

Team cultures and collaboration can work well but should not stifle individualism and the spark of originality. Clearly, collaboration and team spirit work positively, but in certain situations single-mindedness and ego play a pivotal role too.

Business leaders often have to make difficult decisions that do not qualify them for the 'most popular boss of the year' award. This is a lonely and tough position to be in and runs counter to any desire they may have to seek approval and popularity amongst the staff. The relationship-building manager should be careful not to cross the line if a team-focused culture has tipped him or her into some kind of pseudo-psychologist role, listening to problems beyond those of professional concern – which is more common than many care to admit.

More introvert and single-minded leaders will find it easy to stay focused on the goals they want to achieve, but remember you can't do everything alone; a certain amount of collaboration is necessary. But keep things open and honest. People may not like what you have to say, but they will appreciate transparency. Personalities and authenticity are key. There is no point in you as a business leader trying to be something you are not, people are not stupid and quickly distrust the phoney.

For a company to thrive, a range of personalities are useful, so let's try to avoid over-reliance on team culture and thinking negatively about those who appear selfish, and appreciate that sometimes individualism is just what we need to foster. Balance is the key.

Becoming influential – vision-based leadership vs values-based leadership

Many people think that to become an influential leader you need to be visionary, have big audacious ideas, inspire and galvanise your team into energetic action. This works for some, but it is not a prerequisite for becoming an influential leader.

You don't have to be a visionary to be an influential leader, but you need to hire well.

If you have worked on the problem solving and decision making chapters for yourself and your teams you have probably recognised that you may have in your midst people with great ideas and visions. This is to be nurtured not feared. In this scenario, you can be a values-based leader. A person who can shape and put into context the ideas which can spring from an inspired team of people.

Innovation doesn't have to come from an influential leader, it can come from any employee who has ideas and is confident in telling you about them. In a similar vein to action step 3 in Chapter 3, the trick is to listen, put them at their ease, discuss at length, adapt accordingly and praise them in a manner that suits them – some will want public accolades while others will just want a handshake and a thank you; it is worth finding out their preferences.

As an influential leader you can lead from behind, monitoring, nurturing and encouraging, with one eye on the marketplace and where you need to be at any given time. Value-based leadership is something that can be improved upon with experience, open-mindedness and a little direction. Are you that person?

To be an influential leader with integrity and with strong people around you, must surely be the most stress-free way to go to work, don't you think? And so we come to the last set of action steps on your journey through *Your Brain is Boss*.

Action steps: how to become a person of influence

1. Encourage a culture of altruism by looking for opportunities to help one another.

2. Be of service to your customers and clients, even if it doesn't directly benefit your business today. It will over time.

3. Being kind to others works, but so does being kind to yourself. Congratulate yourself when you have done something you are proud of.

4. Success is all about relationships. Take someone out for coffee, go for a walk for your meeting, ask them about themselves.

5. Get into the habit of showing people you trust them, but make sure they have the resources to do what you ask.

6. If someone trusts you and you make a mistake, immediately apologise and offer to make amends.

7. Go out of your way to be trustworthy: do what you say you are going to do when you say you are going to do it. Never fail.

8. Always follow up immediately after you have met someone. Become that person of integrity.

9. If people don't live up to your standards, don't worry, there won't be many like that.

10. If you are building relationships, keep it professional, but warm and authentic.

11. If you are not an innovator, hire an innovator. If you are not an ideas person, hire an ideas person.

12. Make time to listen properly. Find out how different people respond to encouragement and act accordingly.

13. Be open-minded and next time someone does well, tell them.

Conclusion

In working with this book you will have armed yourself and others with a range of tools that will make for success, health, wealth and wellbeing. The phrase 'your brain is boss' is still true, but you are now in better control than you were before.

May I suggest you revisit some of the chapters when you need them? And in going over the material again, you are likely to see something different as you need it.

If you want to discuss anything within or related to this book, please feel free to email me via my website drlyndashaw.com I'm always keen to hear from people with ideas, challenges or feedback.

May your life be full of exciting opportunities as the years unfold.

I wish you all the luck in the world.

Reading list

Chapter 1 The foundation

Ekman, P. (2016) *Nonverbal Messages: Cracking the code: My life's pursuit*. Paul Ekman Group.

Gerace, A., Day, A., Casey, S. and Mohr, P. (2013) 'An exploratory investigation of the process of perspective taking in interpersonal situations'. *Journal of Relationships Research* 4.

Gordon, I.E. (1989) *Theories of Visual Perception*. Guildford, UK: John Wiley & Sons Ltd.

Koch, C. (2004) *The Quest for Consciousness: A neurobiological approach*. Englewood, CO: Roberts & Company Publishers.

Mennella, J.A. and Beauchamp, G.K. (1996) 'The early development of human flavor preferences'. In E.D. Capaldi (ed.), *Why We Eat What We Eat: The psychology of eating*. Washington, DC: American Psychological Association, USA.

Shaw, L.J. (2008) 'Emotional processing of natural images in brief exposures and compound stimuli: fMRI and behavioural studies'. Available at: http://bura.brunel.ac.uk/handle/2438/3203.

Chapter 2 Getting fit for the job

Garth, M. (1991) *Starbright: Meditations for children*. New York: HarperCollins.

Lazar, S. (2011) *How meditation can reshape our brains*. TED Talk, Cambridge. Available at: https://www.youtube.com/watch?v=m8rRzTtP7Tc.

Rani, N.J. and Rao, P.V.K. (1996) 'Meditation and attention regulation'. *Krishna Journal of Indian Psychology* 14(1–2): 26–30.

Ratey, J. and Hagerman, E. (2009) *Spark! How exercise will improve the performance of your brain*. London: Quercus.

Rath, T. and Harter, J. (2010) *Wellbeing*. New York: Gallup Press.

Ren, J., Huang, Z., Luo, J., Wei, G., Ying, X., Ding, Z., Wu, Y. and Luo, F. (2011) 'Meditation promotes insightful problem-solving by keeping people in a mindful and alert conscious state'. *China Life Sciences* 54(10): 961–965.

Sapolsky, R. (1994) *Why Zebras Don't Get Ulcers*. New York: W.H. Freeman & Co.

Sobolewski, A., Holt, E., Kublik, E. and Wróbel, A. (2011) 'Impact of meditation on emotional processing: A visual ERP study'. *Neuroscience Research* 71(1): 44–48.

Chapter 3 Upgrade your skills

Beldoch, M. (1964) 'Sensitivity to expression of emotional meaning in three modes of communication'. In J.R. Davitz *et al.* (eds.), *The Communication of Emotional Meaning* (pp. 31–42). New York: McGraw-Hill.

Bradberry, T. and Greaves, J. (2009) *Emotional Intelligence 2.0*. TalentSmart USA.

Caruso, D.R. and Salovey, P. (2004) *The Emotionally Intelligent Manager*. New York: Jossey-Bass.

Gardner, H. (1983) *Frames of Mind: The theory of multiple intelligences*. New York: Basic Books.

Goleman, D. (1995) *Emotional Intelligence: Why it can matter more than IQ*. London: Bloomsbury Publishing.

Goleman, D., Boyatzis, R.E., McKee, A. (2002) *The New Leaders*. London: Little, Brown.

Goleman, D. (2006) *Social Intelligence*. London: Hutchinson.

Grandey, A.A., Diefendorff, J.M. and Rupp, D.E. (2013) *Emotional Labor in the 21st Century: Diverse perspectives on emotional regulation at work*. New York: Routledge.

Leuner, B. (1966) 'Emotional intelligence and emancipation'. *Praxis der Kinderpsychologie und Kinderpsychiatrie* 15: 193–203.

Matthews, B. (2006) *Engaging Education: Developing emotional literacy, equity and co-education*. Buckingham, UK: McGraw-Hill/Open University Press.

Salovey, P. and Brackett, M.A. (2004) *Emotional Intelligence: Key readings on the Mayer Salovey model*. New York: Dude Publishing.

Steiner, C. (2003) *Emotional Literacy: Intelligence with a heart*. Chicago, IL: Personhood Press.

Chapter 4 Becoming exceedingly valuable

Guilford, J.P. (1950) 'Creativity'. *American Psychologist* 5: 444–454 .

Ohlsson, S. (1992) 'Information processing explanations of insight and related phenomena'. *Advances in the Psychology of Thinking* 1: 1–44.

Poincaré, H. (1913) *The Foundations of Science* (G.H. Halstead, trans.). New York: Science Press.

Saggar, M., Quintin, E.M., Kienitz, E., Bott, N.T., Sun, Z., Hong, W., Chien, Y., Liu, N., Dougherty, R.F., Royalty, A., Hawthorne, G. and Reiss, A.L. (2015) 'Pictionary-based fMRI paradigm to study the neural correlates of spontaneous improvisation and figural creativity'. *Scientific Reports* 5, Article number: 10894.

Simonton, D.K. (1999) *Origins of Genius: Darwinian perspectives on creativity*. New York: Oxford University Press.

Wallas, G. (1926) *The Art of Thought*. London: Cape.

Weisberg, R.W. (2006) *Creativity: Understanding innovation in problem solving, science, invention and the arts*. New York: Wiley.

Chapter 5 Powering up

Anderberg, R.H., Hansson, C., Fenander, M., Richard, J.E., Dickson, S.L., Nissbrandt, H., Berqquist, F. and Skibicka, K.P. (2015) 'The stomach-derived hormone ghrelin increases impulsive behavior'. *Neuropsychopharmacology* 41(5): 1199–1209.

Damasio, A.R. (1994) *Descartes' Error: Emotion, reason and the human brain*. New York: Putnam's & Sons.

Damasio, A.R. (1996) 'The somatic marker hypothesis and the possible functions of the pre-frontal cortex'. *Transactions of the Royal Society* (London) 351: 1413–1420.

Damasio, A.R. (2001) 'Fundamental feelings'. *Nature* 413(6858): 781.

Gigerenzer, D., Todd, P.M. and ABC Groups (eds.) (1999) *Simple Heuristics That Make Us Smart*. New York: Oxford University Press.

Kahneman, D. (2011) 'Introduction'. *Thinking, Fast and Slow*. New York: Farrar, Straus and Giroux.

Kihlstrom, J.F. (2010) 'Unconscious processes'. In D. Reisberg (ed.), *Oxford Handbook of Cognitive Psychology*. New York: Oxford University Press.

Klein, G. (2004) *The Power of Intuition: How to use your gut feeling to make better decisions at work*. Penguin Random House.

Simon, H.A. (1957) *Models of Man*. New York: Wiley.

Chapter 6 Enhancing your communication skills

Seligman, M.E.P. (2003) *Authentic Happiness: Using the new positive psychology to realise your potential for lasting fulfilment*. Boston, MA: Nicholas Brealey Publishing.

Seligman, M.E.P. (2011) *Flourish: A new understanding of happiness and well-being – and how to achieve them*. Boston, MA: Nicholas Brealey Publishing.

Chapter 7 Boosting your message

Damasio, A. (2000) *The Feeling of What Happens: Body, emotion and the making of consciousness*. London: Vintage Books.

Chapter 8 The ultimate goal

Benson, P.L., Clary, E.G. and Scales, P.C. (2007) 'Altruism and health: Is there a link during adolescence?' In S.G. Post (ed.), *Altruism and Health: Perspectives from empirical research*. New York: Oxford University Press.

Dawson, T.M. and Snyder, S.H. (1994) 'Gases as biological messengers: Nitric oxide and carbon monoxide in the brain'. *The Journal of Neuroscience* M(9): 5147–5159.

Gallup survey (2017) 'How engaged is your remote workforce?' *Business Journal* 22 March 2017.

Hamilton, D. (2010) *Why Kindness is Good for You*. London: Hay House UK.

Lieberman, M.D. (2013) *Social: Why our brains are wired to connect*. Oxford University Press.